Rights, Wrongs, & In-Betweens

Guiding Our Children to Christian Maturity

Jim Larson

AUGSBURG Publishing House • Minneapolis

To Jill,
with love and gratitude

RIGHTS, WRONGS, AND IN-BETWEENS
Guiding Our Children to Christian Maturity

Copyright © 1984   Augsburg Publishing House

Scripture quotations unless otherwise noted are from the Holy Bible: New International Version. Copyright 1978 by the New York International Bible Society. Used by permission of Zondervan Bible Publishers.

Library of Congress Cataloging in Publication Data

Larson, Jim, 1942-
    RIGHTS, WRONGS, AND IN-BETWEENS.

    Bibliography: p. 142
    1. Christian education of children.   2. Christian ethics—Study and teaching.   3. Moral education.
4. Values.   5. Family—Religious life.   I. Title.
BV1475.2.L34   1984   248.8'4   83-72121
ISBN 0-8066-2065-X (pbk.)

Manufactured in the U.S.A.   APH   10-5518

1   2   3   4   5   6   7   8   9   0   1   2   3   4   5   6   7   8   9

Contents

Preface

Not many years ago, life seemed pretty simple when it came to values. Values were often very clear and specific. And a system of values was usually passed on from generation to generation without much question or hesitancy.

But in recent generations life has become much more complicated. Many things that were once taken for granted have been challenged. What once seemed black and white now appears very gray. Today we talk more about "in-betweens" than we do about rights and wrongs.

Did you know that:

- roughly three-fourths of our human knowledge has been learned since World War II?
- it is estimated that we will increase our knowledge six times over in the next 35 years?
- by the time children born in the 1970s reach age 50, 97% of all human knowledge will have been learned since they were born?

Not only are we confronted by a revolution of accelerating knowledge and technology, but we are surrounded by conflicting value systems that cry out to be accepted.

- The number of new religious groups has risen significantly in recent years.
- Seductive advertising is used to sell everything from cars to perfume, clothing, and food.
- Some rock singers and other entertainers live out a life-style which assumes that immorality and unfaithfulness are not only permissible, but should be flaunted.
- Cheating, lying, and stealing are often rationalized as all right because "everyone does it."

And to complicate matters further, confusion results from more than just the conflict between secular and Christian values. There is often disagreement among Christians as to what constitutes Christian values. Interpretations of key scripture passages and traditions vary widely, each group loudly insisting that it is the upholder of orthodoxy.

In the midst of all of this change and conflict, perhaps you have experienced times, as I have, of feeling confused, perplexed, even overwhelmed.

At times, we may feel as if we're maneuvering a small tugboat through a horrendous hurricane, a storm in which only the largest ships can survive. And there we are, tossed by the waves like a dead leaf, buffeted by a howling wind, and blinded by the rain. The effort needed to survive may be exhausting.

With the pressures of survival pressing in on us, with the uncertainties which come economically, relationally, and vocationally, we may wonder if we have the strength to deal adequately with the vital moral issues that we face.

The goal of this book is to clarify and deal with various issues related to rights and wrongs, including guidelines for dealing with the many "in-betweens" we confront every day.

This book is designed not only to provide you with reading materials related to values and the family, but to give suggestions for implementing these materials with your family. Be sure to read and experiment with the suggestions provided at the end of each chapter.

As we share together through this book, perhaps we can achieve a greater sense of confidence and calm as we seek to be the kind of parents God wants us to be, guiding our children to moral and spiritual maturity.

Jim Larson

Part 1

Values and Development

What are values?
How are values different from morals?
Are values possessed from birth?
Do values control our thoughts and actions?
Can values be taught?
Do they ever change?
How do self-esteem and other aspects of development (including social and intellectual aspects) affect one's developing values?
How are the values of young children different from those of teenagers?
Do parents really have much influence on their children's values?
Why should parents be aware of their own values?

1

What Is a Value?

Have any of these situations ever happened in your family?

MOTHER   Now, Suzie, I want you to wear your new blue sweater to preschool today. It's such a pretty sweater.

SUZIE   I don't want to wear that yucky blue sweater. I *hate* blue! I want to wear my yellow one.

MOTHER   Suzie, you know that you've never worn your blue sweater. And your grandmother made it especially for you. She would be so sad if she knew you wouldn't wear that sweater.

SUZIE   I don't *care*. I don't *want* to wear it. I don't *like* it!

MOTHER   *(Sigh.)*

FATHER   Billy, it's time to go to Sunday school. Hurry and get dressed.

BILLY   Oh, dad, I don't want to go to church today.

FATHER   Why not?

BILLY   Well, it's kind of boring. I don't know any other kids from my school. I'd just like to stay home.

FATHER   But it's good for you to go, Billy. You learn lots of good things that can help you in life. And . . . .

BILLY   I don't want to go, Dad. I really want to stay home!

FATHER   Billy, you're going to go, so let's stop arguing about it!

BILLY   Why do I have to go? You don't go very often.

ALLISON   Mom, can I go to a slumber party at Stephanie's Friday night?

MOTHER   Sounds like a lot of fun. Who will be there?

ALLISON   Well, quite a few of my friends from eighth grade are invited. We'll be swimming for a few hours. I guess Stephanie has invited some boys to be there, too, but they will be leaving before midnight.

MOTHER   Midnight? Isn't that kind of late? What do Stephanie's parents think about that?

ALLISON   Well, they don't mind. Stephanie gets to have late parties there all the time. And, besides, her parents won't even be there. They'll be out of town for the weekend.

MOTHER   You mean there won't be any adults at Stephanie's during the evening or overnight?

ALLISON   I guess not. But nobody will get in trouble.

MOTHER   I don't feel too good about that.

ALLISON   Why not?

MOTHER   I feel there should be at least one adult there, or else I don't want you to go.

ALLISON   *(heatedly)*   You never trust me, mother. When are you going to let me grow up? I can handle myself! *(Allison slams the door as she leaves the room.)*

Beginning with the youngest child, parents frequently find themselves confronted by conflicts and concerns, both large and small, with their children. And often at the root of these conflicts is a disagreement over values.

Just as God created each one of us as special, unique people, so we differ to some extent in our values.

It is important for us to explore in some depth what values are, and how they influence our actions and feelings. That's what this chapter is about.

What Is a Value?

Webster defines a value as "relative worth, utility, or importance; something intrinsically valuable or desirable." In other words, a value is something that is very important.

A moral is a principle of right or wrong. So, moral development is the development of feelings and attitudes regarding what is right or wrong. And it is often our values—what we consider to be of great importance—that influence our feelings regarding rightness or wrongness for us in any situation.

God has created every person to be a valuing creature. We all prefer some things in terms of usefulness or general worth over others. We can know and feel; we can also value.

Values can be expressed in everything from preference in foods to tastes in music, politics, friends, careers, leisure activities, and religious beliefs.

And values do not seem to be established permanently in life, never to be modified or changed. As people grow and mature, so do their values and preferences. What a person values one year may or may not be exactly what is important the next.

Some parents may be frightened by what they see as the decline or disintegration of traditional values, especially if their children question these values or choose alternative values. In our society today, we are confronted by divergent and contradictory values every place we look—in newspapers, magazines, radio and television, and sports.

And since values are so vital for healthy development and mature behavior, parents are usually concerned about the values that their children develop.

Values: Words or Actions?

One of the important questions we need to deal with is: What reveals our values—our words regarding what we say we value, or our actions?

There are many people who may *say* they have certain values and openly profess them. But people do not necessarily act on these verbalized values. For example, one man may *say* he believes in racial equality, but if a person of a race different from his own attempts to move next door to him, he may oppose such a move with deeply felt racism.

So a person may state a preference or belief, but it may not always be actualized in behavior.

Values expressed in behavior, on the other hand, go a step further than spoken values, since action is involved. For example, a woman who smokes may verbally express a preference for stopping smoking—a spoken value. But if she actually stops smoking, she has expressed another level of value—that of behaviorally expressed values.

When we consider moral development, we need to rely on more than words. How a person behaves shows what he or she ultimately sees as being of greatest importance.

14

Values and Faith

Jesus Christ talked about the importance of our attitudes and actions in a slightly different way: "By their fruit you will recognize them. Do people pick grapes from thornbushes, or figs from thistles? Likewise every good tree bears good fruit, but a bad tree bears bad fruit" (Matt. 7:16-17). In other words, the quality of the "fruit"—our attitudes and actions—will reflect the thoughts and beliefs that come from within.

The apostle Paul expressed a similar thought when he said: "And this is my prayer: that *your love may abound more and more* in knowledge and depth of insight, so that you may be able to discern what is best and may be pure and blameless until the day of Christ, filled with the fruit of righteousness that comes through Jesus Christ—to the glory and praise of God" (Phil. 1:9-11).

And James also clearly stated the importance of works (actions) as well as faith (beliefs, values) when he said: "But someone will say, 'You have faith; I have deeds.' Show me your faith without deeds, and I will show you my faith by what I do. . . . As the body without the spirit is dead, so *faith without deeds is dead*" (James 2:18, 26).

Values, then, are very important to us. They are our preferences, our likes and dislikes, which make us who we are. Values heavily influence our actions, as well as our thoughts and feelings.

As Christians, we need to remember that we can have values that the Scriptures teach us, values that our Savior Jesus Christ wants our families to use as our guides for living.

In the midst of a world that seems to have so many contradictory values, a world without a clear sense of direction regarding what is right or wrong, loving or unloving, we need to ask ourselves questions such as the following:

- How do values develop?
- What is my role as parent in the development of values in my children?
- What do I personally value?
- What is our source of authority when it comes to determining Christian values?
- How can I teach values effectively in the family?

My hope is that the following chapters will be both helpful and stimulating to you as you clarify your own values and discover ways to teach values to your children that are both practical and relevant.

Your Turn

1. Scripture Search

The Scriptures have a great deal to teach us about values. As a starting point, read the following passages to discover what are some significant values to God.

Matt. 6:26
Matt. 12:12
Matt. 13:45-46
1 Tim. 4:4-8

2. Values in Society

Take a few minutes to glance through a current magazine, or watch an hour of television. Make a list of the kinds of values you see expressed in advertising.

3. Values and Conflict

In the next several days, be especially aware of any

conflicts you have with your children. In what ways are values involved in these conflicts? At these points of conflict (which happen in every family), identify how your values differ from those of your children.

2

What's Developing?

Father and two-year-old Susan have stopped at the supermarket for some milk and bread. They have to hurry, since dinner is almost ready at home.

As the pair dashes through the store—with father pulling at Susan's reluctant arm—suddenly Susan stops dead in her tracks. "Candy! I want candy!"

"Susan," her father says in a whispering voice. "It's almost dinner time. If you eat candy now, you won't want to eat your dinner."

"I'm hungry!" Susan persists. *"I want a caaandy baaar!"*

As a gathering crowd watches the confrontation with growing interest, Susan's father mutters, "Why can't you understand? We'll be eating dinner in a few minutes! Just be more patient!"

Have you ever found yourself wondering why your child does not seem to understand? Or can't wait just a few minutes? Or why your child clings to you one day, and the next day doesn't want to be seen in the same city with you? Or persists with complaints that something you did wasn't fair?

Does all of this leave you perplexed? If so, take heart! We're about to deal with the dynamics which can most influence these changes and perplexities.

Each Child Is Unique, But . . . .

There is no doubt that in many ways, each of our children is unique—in looks, temperament, feelings, ways of coping with stress, intellectual capacity, and so on. In fact, as I was reminded years ago in a college textbook, children of the same parents may have any of *280 billion* different chromosome combinations! What an incredible amount of potential differences there can be even within the same family!

An important way in which people are different from each other is the *rate* of their growth and development.

Researchers in human development tell us that we all go through similar processes as we grow from infancy through the adult years. And these steps of growth seem to take place in a certain order.

For example, most young children sit up before they crawl, and crawl before they walk. (Although a few children in recorded history have been known to *run* before they crawl or walk!)

But the *rate* at which children venture along their developmental pilgrimages varies from child to child. It is as if each child has an "inner clock" which affects the rate of development.

For this reason, we need to remind ourselves as parents to be careful about comparing our children, or comparing our children with someone else's.

You've probably been at a social gathering, as I have, where the conversation went something like this: "I'm so thrilled! Jeff just rolled over—and he's only three months old. I can tell that it will be just a matter of days before he can pull himself up. How old was your child when he could roll over?"

"Well," I mumbled, "I don't quite remember. Maybe about five months."

"Oh, really? That's quite late, isn't it? Maybe you should have your child checked by your doctor."

In our hurry-up-and-get-everything-done-fast culture, we may fall into the trap of believing that speed is the key ingredient for superior development.

Certainly it is true that markedly retarded development may signal that something is seriously wrong. But there is a normal range of growth and development that allows for great latitude in terms of the *rate* of development—even among children in the same family.

Just as there are time zones such as Eastern, Central, Mountain, and Pacific, so there is a variety of "time zones" within children as to the rate at which they develop.

Keep this in mind the next time you feel tempted to compare one child's growth with another.

Factors Influencing the Development of Values

Values do not develop in a vacuum. In fact, their development is greatly affected by everything we are and experience—our bodies, thoughts, feelings, relationships, attitudes toward ourselves and others, and so on. So, as we determine how to guide our children in the development of values, we need to identify the other areas of development that have the most direct bearing on values.

Self-Esteem: The Foundation of Growth

According to *Webster's New Collegiate Dictionary,* the word *esteem* means worth; value; high regard. To esteem someone or something means to set a high value, to regard it highly and prize it accordingly.

When we think of self-esteem, we are considering the value or worth one attributes to oneself—whether positive, neutral, or negative.

Self-esteem is like looking into an inner mirror. We see an image of ourselves (self-concept). But how do we feel about what we see in that mirror? Is that person attractive? Loveable? Wanted? Capable? Or ugly? Incompetent? Clumsy? That is self-esteem.

Self-esteem is not completely apparent at birth but develops over a lifetime. It is not an absolute that is always high or low, totally adequate or inadequate for all time. Self-esteem exists on a pendulum which can vary from year to year and circumstance to circumstance.

But there does seem to be a basic self-concept that develops quite early in life and may exist in that form for many years—even throughout one's entire life. And this basic sense of self is one of the most powerful determinants of a person's destiny.

An extreme example is that of an actor I read about who grew up in an abusive environment. For years, his parents told him that he was dumb and stupid. He was even institutionalized for a time for supposedly being mentally retarded.

The tragedy was that his parents did not understand that their child's "inner clock" of growth was just slower than most. He was not, in fact, retarded.

But being a vulnerable young child, he believed his parents. He absorbed the belief that he was dumb, and he needed years of work for his self-concept to become more positive.

He did not finish first grade until he was 26. But once he realized that he had been living according to a myth

21

all of his life, he was determined to "catch up" on all he had missed as a child.

With the encouragement of friends and the help of therapists, this man has been able to modify his self-concept to be a realistic reflection of who he really is. And today he is leading a creative and happy life.

There are many factors that influence the development of self-esteem:

- the parent's expectations for the child
- the quality of relationships within the family
- feelings about the family's economic situation
- attitudes of brothers, sisters, and other family members
- the rate of biological maturation—whether a child is an "early bloomer," within the average range, or a "late bloomer"
- the opinion of peers
- experiences and demands of school, and so on.

Why is it that healthy self-esteem is so important for positive development?

1. *People who feel good about themselves can invest their energies creatively on what is worthwhile.*

Think of creative energy as something like fuel—a quantity of something needed to keep us moving, like oil or gas are needed as energy to keep our homes heated or cars functioning.

Just as there is a limit to the amount of fuel available on earth, so there is a limit to the creative energy we have.

People who do not see themselves as adequate or love-able often have to spend much of their time and energy covering their inferior feelings by being defensive, overcompensating, bitter, or whatever. And that takes a lot of energy!

When that happens, there is little energy left for enjoying life—for appreciating oneself and others, or for coping with the stresses of life.

2. *A person's behavior becomes consistent with the concept of self.*

As the Scriptures tell us, "As he thinks within himself, so he is" (Prov. 23:7). Persons who see themselves as inferior, for example, will usually act in inferior ways—by apologizing, failing, feeling miserable. In this way, they actually do seem to have problems of inferiority.

Thus, a vicious cycle begins—a person feeling inferior, acting in "inferior" ways, getting awkward responses from others, who thus inadvertently reinforce the feelings of inferiority the person felt in the first place.

Children who see themselves as inadequate academically tend to be afraid of trying new tasks and taking tests.

On the other hand, children who tend to feel more adequate and realistic about their abilities tend to be more confident about trying new tasks. In that way, they tend to be more successful.

3. *Persons with healthy self-esteem tend to have happier relationships with others.*

Persons with healthy esteem usually are not held back by fears of rejection or do not need to lash out aggressively to cover their sense of inferiority. Instead, energies can be invested in being loving and nurturing as well as being loveable.

We can't share with others what we don't have ourselves. So if we aren't able to accept ourselves and both appreciate our capabilities and accept our limitations, we will tend to act the same way toward others—and thus make meaningful relationships quite difficult, if not impossible.

Social Development: The Bridge to Others

From the very beginning, people have lived most happily in relationships with others. To exist as a recluse who has little or nothing to do with other people is to go against the very grain of our lives.

Learning how to be social—to share, communicate, love, and be loved—is both an art and a science; it is a lifelong process that continues throughout the life cycle, from infancy through adulthood.

From the first day of birth, people need to be close to others. In fact, to deprive a young child of closeness can do permanent harm to the child.

Since children are born into social units we call families, their most formative social learning takes place in those families. Even before words can be spoken, children learn to communicate with their parents and other family members.

Very quickly, parents learn that there are different cries for being hungry, wet, lonely, frightened, or angry. Within a matter of months and years, sounds become words, so that the communication process is greatly improved.

At first, children are greatly dependent on their parents. In fact, the human baby is the most dependent of all mammals in the early years after birth. And this dependency for food and nurture continues for several years.

Children are also emotionally dependent on their parents for love and security in their early years. So when they venture out into the "cold, cruel world" of friends and other adults, they may at times quickly return to the nest for a reassuring hug.

As children learn to play, they tend to play better on their own than with others. In fact, most young children have difficulty playing together.

But through increasing opportunities for play in the preschool years, children learn to play together and share.

As children grow, they become more capable of having empathy toward others—to understand their feelings and needs, and to see the consequences of their actions on other people. They learn how to give love as well as receive it. In this way, the ability to have friends and be friends becomes easier with age for most children.

A child's social development is an important factor for developing values. For example, a child who has not learned how to share will tend to be quite egocentric when it comes to making decisions regarding what is good or bad, right or wrong, especially when considering the needs or interests of others.

Some children remain dependent long after they should learn to become more independent. In making decisions regarding values, such children may use the opinions of their friends as the sole reason for a particular choice. As children learn to become more independent, they can consider the opinions of their friends but learn to make choices that may not always be popular.

Intellectual Development: The Door to the Mind

Intellectual development is the growth of the ability to reason or think—to know. It centers mainly in the development of the brain, but is influenced by the maturation of the nervous system, relationships with family and friends, pressures to grow, and interaction with one's surroundings. And besides all of that, we have been created with a general tendency to organize what we experience—to structure it in ways that make life understandable.

As with other phases of development, the process of growing intellectually is remarkably similar for most children, even though the rate of development does vary widely from child to child. In fact, there is perhaps no other area of growth with such a wide range of individual differences than intellectual development. Even within a single age level, there may be a several-year variance in language and reading ability.

When we talk about intellectual development, we are really considering several dimensions, including one's relationship to space and time, language and reading ability, and imagination.

Researcher Jean Piaget has discovered that there are several stages children experience as they grow intellectually:[1]

Sensorimotor or Action Intelligence Stage
(birth to 2 years)

Piaget observed that very young children are learning to coordinate their nerves, senses, and muscles which produce behavior, and that knowledge develops through interaction with people and objects.

One of the major tasks for the infant is establishing the knowledge of the permanence of objects. For example, the infant seems to think that if someone or something is outside of his or her range of vision, the object has disappeared—it has vanished! Gradually, the infant learns that people and objects exist even if they are outside the range of vision.

Children in this stage live in the present. They just cannot wait, sometimes to the consternation of their parents. But Piaget says that the young child's intellectual capacities are so limited that response is only to the now, not what was or is to be.

The newborn communicates at first through crying, but gradually learns to make other sounds like cooing, babbling, and an increasing number of other sounds used to communicate.

Preoperational or Prelogical Stage
(approximately ages 2 to 7)

By this age, children are usually involved enthusiastically in acquiring the skills of language—of communicating through words with other people.

Children at this age continue to be quite literal, factual, and intuitive; for this reason, they still cannot be logical for the most part.

Piaget maintains that the major task of this stage is to establish the knowledge of what he calls *perceptual constancy*. In other words, the child needs to learn that objects and people remain the same, even though they may be seen from a different perspective. For example, the child learns that a person remains the same height, even though that person appears to be smaller when seen from a longer distance.

As children enter school, the opportunities to learn expand greatly.

Concrete Operations Stage (approximately ages 7 to 11)

Once a child has reached this stage, there is increased ability to use reasoning power and symbolic thinking. Children can solve problems, compare, contrast, and see similarities and differences in ways the younger child could not experience.

There is often an increasing consciousness of time, with anxiety about being late for school or other obligations.

The desire to read, to listen, and to think is also growing at this age.

Formal Operations or Abstract Thinking Stage
(approximately ages 11 through adult)

By age 11 or 12, many children are learning to think more abstractly and logically. There are often moral questions regarding fairness, rightness, and wrongness.

It is at this age that children can grapple with complex questions such as: What is the purpose of life? Why do bad things happen to good people? Where is God in all of this? What is the difference between right and wrong?

Because of the development of the brain and nervous system, it is quite difficult, if not impossible, for children to deal with such abstract questions until they are at least in the upper elementary grades.

We need to remember the characteristics of these stages of intellectual growth when we find ourselves feeling perplexed as to why our children don't seem to understand what we are talking about.

Remember, there is an "inner clock" that is guiding this entire miraculous process, and when the time is right, our children will be capable of dealing with the rights, wrongs, and in-betweens of life in ways that will astound us.

Moral Development: Setting Standards of Right and Wrong

A researcher who has greatly helped us to understand how moral development takes place is Lawrence Kohlberg of Harvard University.

Dr. Kohlberg has conducted his research in several

countries and cultures, and he has concluded that people everywhere develop through the same process: Children grow from making moral judgments in terms of immediate external physical consequences to judging in terms of internal purposes, norms, and values. Becoming moral, then, means that a person becomes increasingly more *inner*-directed (personal attitudes and values) than *outer*-directed (external laws or expectations).

He has concluded that just as people grow through a series of stages of intellectual growth, so they also develop through a series of moral stages that are in a predetermined sequence.[2] A person may stop growing at any of the stages, and very few people seem to achieve the highest stage of moral development. Movement from stage to stage seems to take place as persons look for more adequate ways to resolve dilemmas as to what is right or wrong, most appropriate or least appropriate.

Kohlberg has identified six moral stages within three general levels:

Level 1: Preconventional Level

At this initial level, a child is primarily concerned about external happenings, especially rewards and the avoidance of punishment.

Stage 1: Punishment and Obedience (ages 5 to 8). At the "Punishment and Obedience" stage the child is concerned about the physical consequences of action, regardless of the meaning or value of these consequences. There is strong motivation to avoid punishment, as well as an unquestioning deference to power and authority.

For example, if a child is caught taking a forbidden cookie from the cookie jar, the action is seen as wrong by the child. But if the child is able to escape detection for the action, the attitude at Stage 1 may be, "Since I did not get caught, what I did was right."

Stage 2: Instrumental Relativist (ages 7 to 10). In this stage, action is motivated by desire for reward or benefit. Thus, what is right is what meets one's own needs and occasionally the needs of others. There is much egocentrism. The attitude is often one of, "I'll help you if you'll help me," rather than a selfless concern to help others.

Level 2: Conventional Level

Kohlberg describes the Conventional Level as that at which maintaining the expectations of one's family, group, or nation is of great value in its own right, regardless of the consequences. There is a strong motivation to conform to what is expected, to perform what is perceived to be good or right roles. Again, there are two stages at the Conventional Level.

Stage 3: "Good Boy—Nice Girl" (ages 10 to 12). At this stage, good behavior is seen as what pleases others, as being approved by them. Children will consequently conform to what they understand is expected by others. One finds approval and is good by being "nice."

Stage 4: Law and Order (ages 12 to 16). At the "Law and Order" stage, the orientation is toward authority and doing one's duty. Actions are usually judged as categorically right or wrong, regardless of motivation or circumstance, since rules are fixed by one's social order and must be maintained no matter what the cost.

Level 3: Autonomous or Principled Level

If a person develops to the Principled Level, moral values become defined by shared standards, rights, and duties—not just by conformity to a standard that someone else imposes.

Stage 5: Social-Contract, Legalistic (early or middle 20s, if ever).   At this stage, right action is seen in terms of individual rights, personal values, and a legal point of view. There is a desire to consider the needs of the larger society and to reach a consensus regarding what should be done.

Thus, personal values, as well as democratically agreed upon goals and values, are of great importance.

An example of people operating at the "Social-Contract" stage, according to Kohlberg, would be America's forefathers. What the early leaders in America did was illegal—they disobeyed the English law that had guided the early colonies. But in their discussion of what was right and moral, the leaders concluded that a new law, one in which people lived in a democracy, was of higher value and needed to be established. So, through a contract, a set of rules embodied in the Constitution, a structure for a new society was established.

Stage 6: Universal-Ethical Principled (late 20s, early 30s, if ever).   A person who achieves this highest level of moral development is concerned not only about laws and regulations, but with *justice,* which Kohlberg maintains is the most important moral principle. For Kohlberg, justice is defined as a respect for persons, as valuing equality in every relationship. To be just is to make moral judgments in terms of what is best for all concerned, rather than on the basis of avoiding punishment, meeting one's own needs, or conforming to a predetermined set of rules.

Whether or not one agrees with Kohlberg's understanding of how moral development takes place, he does provide a helpful structure for seeing how values develop:

- from a concern for avoiding punishment and being rewarded
- to meeting one's own needs exclusively
- to doing only what will be pleasing to others
- to conforming to fixed rules and doing one's duty
- to making justice and equality primary in every moral judgment.

As we have already mentioned, Kohlberg has found that many persons do not move through every moral stage. For example, he has found that many people confined to prison for repeated crimes have never moved beyond Stage 1. And the majority of people seem to stay at the "Law and Order" stage.

Even as we realize that some people do not develop their full capacities as moral people, persons do have potential for moving to a higher level of morality. We can grow beyond being preoccupied with our own needs to understanding the point of view of others—a turning outward to others.

In Conclusion

Are you surprised that the development of values is such an intricate process? Self-esteem and social and intellectual development affect our development of values. We cannot totally separate our developing understanding of right and wrong from how we feel about ourselves in relationship to others, and how we grow in understanding.

As you relate to your children, no matter what their age, remember that *developmental* is the key word we use to describe the process by which we obtain our sense of right and wrong. It doesn't happen overnight, but takes many years to nurture, much like a rare flower bulb that needs tender loving care until full bloom is achieved.

Your Turn

1. Observe your child (or children) in their daily activities and ask yourself the following questions:

• How does your child seem to feel about himself/herself? Is there a healthy sense of self-esteem? Or does your child seem riddled by self-doubts?

• How is your child's self-esteem exhibited in actions?

• How is your child doing socially? Does your child relate well to other children?

• In which stage does your child seem to be intellectually (according to Piaget's stages)? What clues indicate this to be true?

2. Consult with your child's teacher(s) (if in preschool, elementary school, or older) to evaluate your child's intellectual growth. Do the teachers indicate that your child is using much of his or her capacities? What do they suggest would help enhance your child's development intellectually?

3. According to your child's age, develop a brief profile as to what are reasonable expectations, especially regarding social, intellectual, and moral growth. In other words, for the age of your child, what are typical characterisics which indicate where your child is in each of these areas? How does this profile compare with your previous expectations for your child?

3

Am I Really Important?

Have you ever found yourself in one of these circumstances?:

As you leave the house for a social function, your two-year-old tries to push you out the door as she hugs the baby-sitter and says: "Leave, Mommy. I don't need you anymore!"

Or you sit down with your eighth-grade son to talk about the "facts of life," only to hear, "Dad, I've heard all of this already. You're four years too late."

Or your third grader comes and says, "Can I take a special computer class on Saturdays? We'll be learning how to develop our own programs."

Or your child's teacher tells you, "Johnny needs more intellectual stimulation at home. Are you encouraging him to read on his own?"

What a whirlwind we live in today! Preschoolers becoming proficient readers. Elementary-age children operating computers and studying algebra. Junior high people designing projects using solar energy or laser beams, which were unheard of until recent years.

In the midst of this ferment and change, we may question how important we really are as parents. Are we merely custodians of our children until they can function on their own? Are we like air traffic controllers, taxi drivers, garbage collectors, or policemen when relating to our children? Or are there other, more significant ways we influence our children?

A Look Backward

Let's begin our discussion of our importance as parents by taking a brief sweep through recent history to see what has been happening to families.

For over 99% of the time people have existed, they have lived in primarily agricultural settings—on farms, where each family was largely self-sufficient. In these families, all members from young children on up played important productive roles in helping to plant and harvest crops and perform other tasks. Children were often treated like miniature adults, who worked hard as children on the farm and at home until they became adults and were ready to leave home to work on their own.

But over the past few centuries, increasing numbers of people have been moving into cities and towns. By the year 2000, more than two-thirds of the world's people will be living in urban centers.

And study after study substantiates the fact that living in cities often increases the stress levels for people, as they cope with crime, drug abuse, crowded living conditions, pollution, and noise.

Along with this move into the cities has been the development of machines and other technological advances. With these changes, more and more people stopped working at home and went to work in factories and businesses, so that work and family became even more separated.

Today, many children are not even sure what their parents do. Recently, I asked a ten-year-old boy what his father did for a living. His answer was something like this: "Well, I know he drives downtown and gets in an elevator and works on the top floor of a tall building. But I'm not sure what he does there. I saw his desk once. It was stacked with papers. I think he makes a lot of telephone calls and moves the papers around."

Statistically Speaking

Here is a summary of what seems to be happening to today's family:

• Marriage is still an extremely important part of American life; 90-95% of Americans marry at least once. Most people relate marriage to permanence and expect their marriages to last throughout their lifetime.

• Reported marital satisfaction is greatest before children are born and after they leave home. Some studies have shown that raising young children can be a stressful experience, especially in its impact on the parents' marriage. Yet other studies do show that 94% of women and 96% of men report finding parenting usually enjoyable.

• In the past 100 years, there has been a 16-fold increase in the divorce rate. By 1971, the United States had the highest divorce rate among the populous nations of the world.

• It is now estimated that four out of every ten children born in the 1970s will spend part of their childhood in a single-parent family, usually with the mother as the head of the household.

• Approximately 80% of divorced persons eventually remarry, the majority within five years after their divorces.

• In 1800 the average number of children in a family was eight. Today the average is less than two children. The average household has shrunk from five persons in 1910 to three in 1975.

• An increasing number of mothers are returning to work outside the home. In 1948, for example, only 26% of married women with school-age children (and 13% of those with preschool-age children) worked outside the home. By 1976, the proportion had grown to 54% of those with school-age children and 37% of those with preschool-age children.

Changes in Family Function

All of these changes have brought about some significant changes in the function of the family. Among the expectations which have changed are:

Education

Since the time public education was instituted in the 19th century, the family has no longer been responsible for educating its children at home. The school is now seen as the primary educator of our children.

Vocational Training

For the most part, parents are not expected to provide job training for their children before they leave home. We leave this to colleges and vocational schools.

Social Development

Increasing numbers of children spend most of their waking hours in day-care centers and preschools from infancy on. And once they are in school, there are numerous opportunities to participate in activities such as sports and clubs, which become primary socializers of our children.

Religion and Values

For many families, the church is seen as the place for the imparting of religious attitudes, faith, and values. Many parents have taken a distinctly secondary role in the religious education of their children. This is a controversial point (in fact, we will return to this concern several times).

We need to evaluate some of these changes. Perhaps they have not all been for the best, especially those related to values and religion. But what seems to have happened is that many of the traditional functions of the family have been taken over by other institutions, such as schools and churches, that claim to have more technical expertise to serve our children. And in the process, today's parent seems to have a more consultative, one-step-removed function than a direct one.

Today's parent is often more of a coordinator or administrator who has little authority over those with whom the task of raising children is shared. This could cause a parent to feel powerless or unimportant.

Is the Family Here to Stay?

Against a backdrop of these statistics, one could feel discouraged or confused, and perhaps feel that the family is being torn to shreds. Has the family's function been weakened to the point where it can no longer be an effective contributor to the healthy well-being of adults, youth, and children?

Is the family here to stay? Decidedly, yes! Most researchers agree that the family is indeed undergoing significant changes as to its role. But a better substitute for the nurturing of people has never been found.

For better or worse, it seems that both parents and children alike are expecting their families to fulfill their emotional needs.

According to family researcher Kenneth Kenniston:

> With work life highly impersonal, ties with neighbors tenuous, and truly intimate out-of-family friendships rare, husbands and wives tend to put all their emotional hope for fulfillment into their family life. Expectations of sharing, sexual compatibility, and temperamental harmony in marriage have risen as other family functions have diminished.[1]

Maybe this is one reason why divorce has become so common. There seems to be a reduction in the number of bonds that tie a family together. In previous times, primary concern was often with survival—living through famines, wars, and plagues. Even if there was a lack of emotional satisfaction, there was still much that a family had in common. There were lower expectations regarding marriage and family life.

But such high expectations about having all of our needs for love, sharing, and security met by such a small group of people can place an enormous burden on family relationships. What happens when marriage and family relationships are under strain, especially to the breaking point? There may be a temptation to look elsewhere, since there is often so little emotional fulfillment in other areas of life.

Don't get me wrong. Preserving and sustaining a marriage and family is one of the most important tasks a person could ever undertake. But as we observe all of the pressures and dynamics affecting families today, and also remind ourselves of the high expectations we have for our families, maybe we can be more empathic for those who find the strains unbearable.

So What Is the Family For?

Despite these changes and strains, the family is essential for a number of reasons:

1. The family is still the means society uses to preserve its species; it is the way that one generation reproduces the next generation and brings it to maturity.

2. The family is important for social and personal stability—for both parents and children. People without some kind of "family" support network—either their relatives or people who become family—often feel rootless and isolated.

3. The family is the place where people can share intimate and unconditional affection. It is a "nurture center," where children and adults provide affectionate care for each other.

As Kenniston reminds us: "Children need adults who are deeply attached to them. Children need adults who will stick with them not because they are paid to but because they have a profound sense of commitment and love." [2]

What specifically are areas in which parents do have significant impact on their children? Let's look at those aspects of development described in the last chapter—self-esteem, social development, and moral development.

Self-Esteem

We saw in our last chapter that healthy self-esteem has great impact on our behaviors, attitudes, and values.

And the early years of childhood—years when family influence is at its greatest—are the most formative for the development of self-esteem.

Children need to feel wanted and loved by their parents so that they can perceive themselves as both loveable and worthy of love.

I remember our experience at the hospital where our first daughter Jennifer was born. My wife's roommate was a woman who had already had several boys, all of them weighing over ten pounds at birth. She delivered another husky boy about the time we had Jennifer. Her attitude was one of outrage and frustration. She insisted she never wanted any children. In fact, she said she would *pay* anyone to take her children.

I wonder where those boys are now—15 years later. I wonder if they are any more wanted now than they were then. I wonder how their behavior reflects their parents' attitude toward them.

What a contrast this mother's attitude is to the majority of parents who, despite whatever inconveniences and sacrifices involved, are deeply committed to their children and love them.

Through giving children a sense of belonging and being worthwhile and capable, parents encourage them to develop confidence and self-respect in dealing successfully with the changes and stresses of life.

Family researchers have shown that children who live in loving, positive family situations will be more stimulated to grow and learn in healthy ways than children who live in hostile or frightening environments.

Social Development
God created every person with a need for relationships with other people. God said, "It is not good for the man to be alone" (Gen. 2:18).

The family plays a key role in helping children become social persons. A child's first and most formative social learning takes place with the parents in the family. These early experiences are vital in determining that child's attitude toward and expectations of others.

Over the childhood years a growing network of relationships, which extend out from parents to other family members and finally to peers and other people, enhances the lives of children.

It is true that the family generally provides a child's first relationships. And yet, in one sense, the family needs to "work itself out of a job." In other words, one of the main functions of the family is to guide a young child to become more self-reliant, to move beyond the absolute dependence of infancy to the independence of adulthood.

In order for people to become fully functioning adults, they need to become independent, and at the same time be able to develop satisfying relationships with persons outside the family. By maturing from *dependence* to *independence,* persons are best able to become *interdependent*—the healthy combination of self-reliance with mature, loving relationships with other people.

"Letting go" of children—encouraging them to become less dependent and more sociable and self-reliant—is one of the most difficult, yet essential, tasks of parenting.

Moral Development

For centuries the family has been acknowledged as having almost an exclusive responsibility for the development of values for its members. And despite the fact that there are increasing numbers of influences on the moral development of children, family researchers have concluded that the family continues to be the most significant factor in the healthy development of values.

The home environment influences everything from personal tastes and preferences, to attitudes regarding other people, to values regarding all areas of life. Leadership potential and school achievement are also greatly influenced by the family.

Young children usually see parents as powerful people, as those who provide love, security, and direction. Children will often imitate the behavior and attitudes of their parents, since home is the place where they observe values in action in the earliest days of life. (The subject of parents being examples will be discussed in Chapter 9.)

Parents influence their children both by what they say (or do not say) as well as by what they do (or do not do). Because children are such perceptive observers, parental example is a more potent influence than words can ever be.

Spiritual Development

God has created people with a need to be related to God. This "God-shaped vacuum" can be filled only by God through a growing, dynamic relationship.

From the very beginning of biblical history, the family has been seen as the place where the legacy of faith can be shared and reproduced.

In Deuteronomy 4:9-10, we read the following:

> Only be careful, and watch yourselves closely so that you do not forget the things your eyes have seen or let them slip from your heart as long as you live. Teach them to your children and to their children after them. Remember the day you stood before the Lord your God at Horeb, when he said to me, "Assemble the people before me to hear my words so that they may learn to revere me as long as they live in the land and may teach them to their children."

The Scriptures tell us that teaching and learning about spiritual matters was to take place at home in both formal and informal ways:

> These commandments that I give you today are to be upon your hearts. Impress them on your children. Talk about them when you sit at home and when you walk along the road, when you lie down and when you get up. Tie them as symbols on your hands and bind them on your foreheads. Write them on the doorframes of your houses and on your gates (Deut. 6:6-9).

Throughout the Scriptures, the role of parent is upheld as vital, even awesome, as providing both joy and grief (see Prov. 10:1).

Jesus acknowledged the care of children as a primary human duty and expected parents to be sensitive to the needs of their children (see Matt. 7:11; 2 Cor. 12:14; Eph. 6:4).

The Christian family, then, is the place where Christian values can be observed and developed, where love and acceptance can be experienced.

Finally

We have seen that the family has great influence upon Anyone who thinks that parenting is an easy task should all areas of our development as human beings, including the moral and spiritual areas.

The task of being leaders in our families is awesome. Listen to what popular family researcher Virginia Satir says about being a parent:

> I regard this as the hardest, most complicated, anxiety-ridden, sweat and blood producing job in the world. It requires the ultimate in patience, com-

mon sense, commitment, humor, tact, love, wisdom, awareness, and knowledge. At the same time, it holds the possibility for the most rewarding, joyous experience of a lifetime.[3]

God has promised to be with us as parents and help us develop the wisdom to be the kind of parents God wants us to be. God has promised to give us the strength to accomplish all that is involved with being a parent.

Your Turn

1. Reminisce with any elderly members of your family with whom you have contact (grandparents, parents, aunts, and uncles) about your family in previous generations. What was your family like in earlier years? What were some of the particular strains or adjustments that took place (immigration; economic stresses; loss of family members through accident, war, or disease, etc.)? What were some of the highlights of those years?

2. Reflect on the influence your parents have had positively and negatively in your life. How are you like each of your parents? How are you different? How is your style of parenting similar to and different from that of your parents?

3. Plan specific ways to enhance your child's self-esteem by promoting the following:

Worth
Belonging
Competence

4

What Are My Values?

At this point in our discussion of values, I would like to share a personal experience that has radically changed my understanding of values and parenting.

Over ten years ago, I found myself at a point of personal crisis. My effectiveness in my vocation (pastoral ministry) seemed to be crumbling, especially in terms of personal fulfillment for me and for my family. At first, I became physically ill on Sundays, then with more frequency until I was constantly sick—with loss of appetite, nausea, headaches, and insomnia.

Finally, my physician told me I needed to take a medical leave from my job. No physical cause could be found for the illness; it was assumed to be stress.

The guidance of an excellent therapist helped me unravel what I was indeed feeling and experiencing. At first I denied that my job could be causing any stress at all. Because of my feeling of being called by God to pastoral ministry, I had forced myself to believe that I was truly happy in my work. But my stomach said otherwise.

The medical leave certainly provided a helpful break. For the first time since my two young children had been born, I had time to be involved in the daily ups and downs of their lives, the minor crises of parenting (everyone having the flu), and the major ones (brother continually biting sister).

One night, near the end of my one-month leave, I was taking a walk with my children, who were comfortably seated in their stroller. As we went along, I suddenly realized that if I had been well, at that moment I would have been involved in a church meeting. I realized that I was doing exactly what I preferred to do at that time—be with my children and enjoy new discoveries as we walked around the block.

I began to realize that much of what I had been experiencing was a conflict in values. My job expectations at church included long hours and little time at home.

But inside of me, I felt a different set of values—wanting to be involved with my children at this critical time in their lives, and really enjoying the moments of serendipity as well as the grimy realities of parenting.

The more I tried to do both, the more frustrated and disillusioned I became. For me, the moment of truth had arrived, and within the next six months I had made a significant vocational change, one that allowed me to have evenings and weekends with my family—the place and the people with whom I felt I truly belonged.

Times of Moral Conflict

I share this memory not to suggest that a parish pastor cannot have a good home life, but because it points out a significant moral conflict that I experienced. In my head I believed that my most important ministry was with my own family. But needs and aspirations (what I brought to the job) and internal and external expectations (what I thought other people expected of me) squeezed me in a vise until I thought I could no longer breathe.

I realized I was at a point of making a significant moral choice that would affect me for years to come. If I continued on the road I had already chosen (that of committing my energies and time more completely to job than to family), I am convinced that I would be in an entirely different place today. As painful as the decision was, I am grateful beyond words that—for me— the correct choice was made.

All of us find ourselves at such critical points at one time or another in our lives. In those moments of ferment, we may not even be sure what the conflicts really are. I know it was not immediately clear to me what the struggle was really about. Several months of reflection were needed to clarify the issues for me.

But often these crises involve a struggle of values, a conflict that may feel as slight as an irritation or as intense as a world war. The struggles that do involve values can help us clarify what our most important values really are.

It is interesting that in the Chinese language the characters used for the word *crisis* mean two things: first, "pain," "upset," or "danger"; and second, "opportunity for growth."

As we experience value conflicts and crises, remember that despite the pain and danger of those moments, they are a very important way of clarifying, choosing, and moving on with the values we have determined to be right for us.

Kinds of Values

There are several kinds of values that influence the choices we make, as well as our behaviors and attitudes. Dr. Ted Ward, professor and director of the Values Development Education program at Michigan State University, maintains that there are at least three different values: *preferences, investments,* and *patterns.*[1]

Preferences are the most basic and perhaps least complex type of values, and they include our personal tastes regarding food, clothing, colors, or styles of furniture, as well as loyalties to favorite athletic teams, television programs, and so on.

These tastes or preferences tell us, as well as the people around us, much about who we are. Think for a moment about your preferences. What might they indicate to others about who you are and what you value?

Investments, on the other hand, are the ways we use our time, energies, and money—those quantities of things over which we have at least some measure of control.

Two ways to determine a person's investments are to keep a log of how one's time is used and review one's checkbook to see how money has been spent.

Again, think for a moment about your own investments. Where do you seem to be investing most of your time and money? What might this indicate to you and to others about your values?

The third kind of value, according to Dr. Ward, is *patterns.* Over a period of time, our preferences and investments tend to stabilize to the point where we establish certain patterns regarding our values. Our preferences and investments begin to affect our relationships with others, as well as our self-esteem; they affect the kinds of jobs we prefer, the ways we use our leisure time, and so forth.

Making Personal Decisions

Now let me bring all of this back to the point of my personal story. In the midst of my personal crisis I was discovering that my investments of time were imbalanced toward involvement in work. The longer I allowed that imbalance to continue, the more permanent the patterns seemed to be. As I learned to get my fulfillment from my vocation, the investment I was making in my family seemed to diminish.

That's why all of us can profit from occasionally doing an inventory of where we are personally and in regard to family, to be sure that our preferences and investments are resulting in the kind of healthy, mature patterns that are of optimum benefit to us personally as well as to our family relationships.

And that is the purpose of this chapter—to point out that in order for us to be most effective with our children regarding the development of a sound and mature value system, we need to be aware of our own values—and those preferences, investments, and patterns that indicate what our values really are.

As I mentioned in the first chapter, our values are evidenced more by our actions (or inactions) than by our words (or silence).

When it comes to parenting, we really cannot share what we do not ourselves possess. For example, it is impossible for parents who have a very inadequate sense of self-esteem to nurture positive esteem in children, unless the parents are also working actively on improving their own self-esteem.

And it is equally impossible for parents to help their children develop socially if they themselves are withdrawn and not working actively at developing relationships with other people.

When it comes to moral and spiritual development, we as parents cannot teach what we do not personify, at least to some extent. We do need to remind ourselves—especially if we feel that we will never be able to personify what we want our children to value and believe—that we are all in process. None of us has fully arrived in terms of moral and spiritual maturity.

But we need to be working in the same direction as those values we are trying to teach our children. Our children need to see that those values are as important to us personally as they should be to them.

Otherwise we are giving our children double messages: what we are saying with our words about what is important and what our children should value is very different from the message we give with our actions. Family researchers have found that double messages lead only to confusion and ambivalence, if not to emotional dysfunction. In fact, one family counselor calls double messages "crazymaking" because of the confusion they can cause.

Finally

We do not need to feel that we have arrived before we can have positive impact on the developing values of our children. But we do need to be clear in our own minds as to what our values are—or should be—and to intentionally set a course for ourselves that will help us achieve the investments and patterns we so deeply desire for our children.

An important mark of personal and family health is called *congruence*, which Webster defines as "marked or enhanced by harmonious agreement among constituent elements." As applied to the development of values, congruence means that our words and our actions coincide—they *match*.

So as we conclude this first section of the book, take some time to do an inventory of your own personal values. This will help you identify ways you need to grow or change, with the ultimate goal that you speak with one voice through your actions and words.

In a day when our children are hearing so many conflicting moral messages, speaking to our children with congruence is crucial.

Your Turn

1. Think back to your childhood days. Make a list of values you had as a child. (Remember: values are reflected more accurately by actions than by words.) As a child, you probably reflected the values of your parents to a great extent.

Once you have completed that list, read back through it and put a check next to each value that you still maintained as an adolescent (ages 12 to 18). Add any new values that emerged during those years for you. How did the dynamic of growing through puberty affect your values? How dominant was the influence of your friends? How did your parents' influence change during those years?

Now read through your values list one more time. Underline each value you still possess today. And add any new values you have developed as an adult.

Read through your values list one last time. What do you learn about yourself, in terms of growth from childhood into adulthood? What has changed regarding values? What has not changed? How do these values compare and contrast with the kinds of values you desire your children to have?

2. You have already begun a personal evaluation by identifying your preferences, investments, and patterns. After you have listed these items, identify any you want to change or any that are missing and need to be included. How will you change any of these areas?

3. Share your lists with your spouse (if you are a two-parent family) or with a close friend or another adult family member with whom you can feel free to share such personal information. Agree to check in with each other at least once a week to see what progress you are making on changing your values. If appropriate, ask your partner to pray for you regularly, that you will have the strength, courage, and wisdom you need to implement the changes you desire for yourself.

Part 2
Values and Faith

Does our ability to reason really influence our values?
If I feel guilty about something, is it automatically
* wrong?*
What do I do when my thoughts, feelings, and values are
* in conflict?*
How do one's values relate to personal faith in God?
Do the Scriptures give us specific guidelines for every
* situation?*
Or instead do they give us general principles we need
* to work out in each situation?*
What values are indeed eternal (true for all generations)?
Which are temporary and most influenced by culture?
How does a relationship with God affect our values
* and life-style?*
Is busyness in church activities an evidence of spiritual
* growth?*
What's the difference between being person-oriented
* and thing-oriented?*
How are my values affected by this orientation?
Are there really "in-betweens" that are not clearly either
* right or wrong?*
How do I decide between two options that both seem
* to be best, right, and true?*
Or how do I proceed when none of the options seems
* that great?*

5

What Is Our Guide?

I'll never forget it—it was one of those embarrassing, humiliating experiences that ultimately taught me a lesson or two.

I was directing a summer camp in the mountains above Los Angeles. The day before the camp was to begin, the staff gathered for an orientation regarding the schedule and program for the week.

Because of the treacherous terrain surrounding the camp, staff members were reminded repeatedly to watch where they were going. And under no circumstances should they ever venture out at night without a high-powered flashlight to show the way.

Later that evening, during an informal recreational time, several staff members asked me to direct them to the crafts room. Since the path was rather difficult, I decided to show them the way by going with them.

I had walked over that path time and again during the day, so I was sure I could find my way without using my flashlight. (I didn't want to take the time to hike back to my cabin to get it.) As we walked along the dark path, I turned to remind the people to be careful as they rounded the bend because. . . .

You can probably guess the rest of my story. Instead of rounding the path's bend, I walked straight off the edge of a cliff, resulting in a fall of several feet. I landed on my knees, which quickly took on an appearance that more resembled raw hamburger meat.

Walking around the camp all week, with my knees tightly bound in bandages, was a reminder of my negligence. On the last day of camp, the staff lovingly gave me a lantern to use in future emergencies!

How stupid I felt! I knew how important a flashlight was in such a place. But my confidence had become cockiness, which ultimately resulted in a needless and embarrassing accident.

Setting Our Focus

I am sure that you and your children are often confronted by decisions that are far from easy to make. Even though rights and wrongs may sometimes be rather obvious, there are other times when the alternatives are less clear, when there seem to be good reasons for each alternative, or when circumstances are so complex that neither alternative appears to be right or best.

Intelligent, mature choices regarding right and wrong are in fact possible. It is not merely an emotional whim that causes us to do what seems best. But in order to make mature moral choices we need to rely on several sources of guidance.

Basic Sources of Guidance for All of Us

As the psalmist says, we are "fearfully and wonderfully made" (Ps. 139:14). We human beings are not merely a breed of animals, guided only by smell, sight, and instinct. Instead, we have been given amazing gifts, such as our minds, feelings, and consciences—gifts that can give us helpful input when we are faced with moral decisions.

Laws

For many situations, laws have been provided by our society to help us. For example, there are laws that help us remember how fast to drive, laws protecting private property, laws regarding how people get married, divorced, and so on. The law libraries and courts are filled with books that enumerate laws for what seems like every situation.

But there *aren't* laws for everything, so other sources of guidance are needed. Traditions, reason, feelings and needs, intuition, and conscience help us know what to do. They are like the intertwined links shown in the illustration below—not totally separate from each other, but tending to overlap and affect each other.

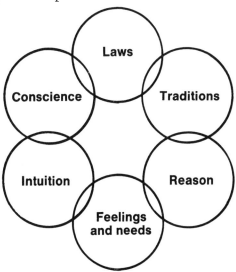

Traditions

Traditions are somewhat different from laws. While laws are usually written and accepted within a society as authoritative, traditions are usually handed down from one generation to another without being written down. They may not even be spoken, but just assumed to be true because they have been customary for so many years.

For example, many nationalities have special ways they celebrate holidays such as Christmas. In my Scandinavian heritage, the main celebration was on Christmas Eve. Christmas Day was a day for quiet relaxation and enjoying one's gifts; Christmas Eve was the time for excitement, opening of presents, and enjoying an extravagant Swedish meal.

Such a tradition was so strong that if a person or family were to decide whether to join the extended family for Christmas Eve or go skiing, there is no doubt which decision would be the "right" one.

Another example is that related to the weaning of young children from nursing or bottle feeding. In some cultures, the tradition is to have several children quite close in age. When a new child is born into a family, the next oldest child, no matter what age, is abruptly terminated from being nursed, no matter how much the child protests. The tradition of the abrupt termination of nursing is so deeply embedded that the idea of a gradual transition from nursing to cup feeding would be strongly resisted.

Traditions can be helpful, especially as related to beliefs or customs, but they can also restrict the options available to those making choices.

Many traditions have an excellent basis for being repeated and honored; others seem to be upheld simply because "we've always done it that way."

Reason

As we have already mentioned, human beings are not guided exclusively by their senses like animals; they also have highly complex brains that allow them to think logically and organize their thoughts.

Through the use of our brains, we can develop *common sense,* which can help us think of the practical aspects of what is right or wrong; *reflection,* which can help us think carefully through complex dilemmas; and *wisdom,* the ability to discern and make wise decisions based on years of experience.

Reason, then, has great potential as a source of guidance for us. But it can also be misused. Some people, even those who are highly intelligent, develop the ability to rationalize or give what seem to be rational reasons for a particular decision.

People frequently rationalize or defend their errors, whether it's a parent who attempts to defend abuse of a child because of alleged misbehavior, a brother who explains why he feels justified to stay alienated from another brother because of a years-old offense, or a person rationalizing feelings of racial hatred.

Even as we acknowledge that reason is an important part of our decision-making process, we need to see how our reasoning can be affected by our needs, feelings, and values. Our reasoning ability is not pure in and of itself; it is greatly affected by these other factors that make us who we are.

Feelings and Needs

Our feelings also have a great impact on our decision-making ability. For example, if our mood is one of joy and confidence—or, on the other hand, one of depression and lack of confidence—those kinds of feelings can affect the decisions we make. If we need to feel powerful, that need, also, may influence a decision we make.

Let me give you an example of how feelings and needs have affected me. At the end of my senior year of college, our class took a special trip (called a "Senior Sneak") away from campus for several days. The object was to get away from campus without being caught by members of the junior class.

We made it successfully off campus and then began a train ride from Illinois to an unknown destination (only our class leaders knew that our exact destination was Colorado).

After traveling several hours, I was asked to make a phone call back to the campus newspaper editor to tell her our destination. She was to share this information in that week's edition of the newspaper.

But to throw the juniors off track—in case they were still looking for us—I was to tell her that we were halfway to Biloxi, Mississippi. I was urged to make the call. "They'll believe you," a class leader maintained.

I was caught in a difficult dilemma. On the one hand, I wanted to tell the truth. Who cared if the rest of the college knew where we were going, anyway? On the other hand, I was at a point in my life where my need to be accepted and included by others made distortion of the truth seem rather inconsequential.

I'm sorry to say that my need for inclusion won out. I made the call, threw the junior class off track, was applauded by my classmates—and felt terrible!

In my head I knew the right choice, but my feelings and needs were so powerful that all rational functioning was set aside.

I share this experience to point out that no matter how intelligent or wise we may feel we are, at times our feelings and needs can be so strong that we allow them to dominate our reason—sometimes to our detriment.

Intuition

Intuition is closely related to feelings; in fact, it is often a vague feeling that something is threatening or wrong or hopeful or right—and is usually not based on reason.

Has this ever happened to you? You take a seat in the personnel office to wait for a job interview. Immediately you have a feeling of discomfort, based not only on nervousness about the interview, but an uncomfortable, anxious feeling that this would not be a good place for you to work.

Or have you ever had feelings that a close friend or relative of yours, who may live thousands of miles away and with whom you have not had frequent contact, is experiencing some kind of difficulty?

That has happened to me several times. I usually follow up those feelings with a phone call. And I have been amazed that on several occasions, something indeed *was* wrong.

I cannot account for those feelings, but I have been amazed how often they have proved to be reliable.

In making decisions about what is right or wrong, we need to listen not only to our feelings and needs, but also to any intuitive feelings we may have regarding the options we are considering.

Conscience

Another source of guidance, one closely related to intuition, is our conscience. Conscience is a built-in guide, an inner voice that arouses feelings and thoughts about the rightness and wrongness of certain behavior.

Conscience often involves feelings of guilt if something "wrong" is done, or even considered. Feeling guilty is a form of self-punishment, a feeling of "Well, you blew it again!" or "How could you do such a dumb thing?"

However, conscience can also involve feelings of joy and fulfillment, that indeed the "right" decision was made.

According to researchers, conscience is often experienced by children as a sense of "mustness," as well as a fear of punishment if something "wrong" is done. Young children see most everything in terms of clear rights and wrongs, with little in-between. Their developing minds cannot discriminate fine points.

But for the adolescent and adult, the conscience becomes a sense of "oughtness," of what *should* be done, rather than what *must* be done. And the mature mind is capable of discriminating more clearly between rights and wrongs, especially the "in-betweens" that often exist between rights and wrongs.

In the book *The Individual and His Religion,* Gordon Allport describes conscience as "the knife-edge that all our values press upon us whenever we are acting, or have acted, contrary to these values." [1]

The conscience is rather mysterious. Where does it come from? Is it merely our parents' code of ethics that we have internalized? Is it the voice of society coming from within? Is it the voice of God? Do our consciences always tell us what is really right? Are the feelings of guilt we experience when we have a "guilty conscience" always appropriate?

People have long wondered about such questions. Certainly our families and our cultures do have a great effect on our developing consciences. That is why, in a particular culture, people may feel guilty about doing something that culture prohibits, while in another culture, no feelings of guilt may result.

We must be cautious, therefore, about identifying our consciences and feelings with God's leading. Just where the two are separated I cannot say for sure. But before we say, "God told me to do that," be sure that you are not speaking only from *your* conscience or feelings.

For the Christian, Added Guidance

Our traditions, reason, feelings, needs, intuitions, and consciences are certainly of great help as we face moral dilemmas. These sources of guidance are available to everyone.

But for Christians there are some additional sources of guidance that can validate the other sources and give greater depth and insight into the entire process of decision making.

Relationship with Jesus Christ

As believers, we have opportunity to live in a growing relationship with Jesus Christ, God's Son.

Our priorities and values change as we put God in the center of our lives. As we confront a myriad of conflicts and dilemmas, we know that we are not alone; God is with us and clearly wants to guide us (see Ps. 94:14).

One of the exciting things about believing in a personal God is that God is not just a God "out there" someplace in the universe, but a God who wants to become integrated into our lives. We have a source of strength for dealing with the strains and challenges of life. We do not become totally freed from the tug of self-centeredness that seeks to make us the center of our personal universe, but we have a resource of help to deal with these pulls and tugs.

As we become believers, we seek to follow Jesus Christ and live according to his teachings. We reorder our priorities so that our actions become based more on God's love and grace and less on personal feelings. Our

65

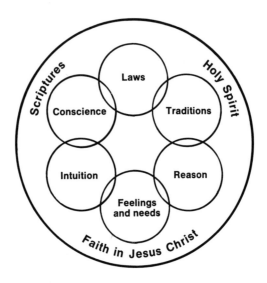

faith in Christ becomes the core of our being and begins to influence and infiltrate our reasoning abilities, feelings, intuition, conscience, and even our traditions (see diagram).

Speaking for myself, I have found that being a follower of Jesus Christ has given me a greater sense of equilibrium and balance, an ability to deal more flexibly with the dilemmas that can so easily throw me off balance. My relationship has pulled many loose ends together into a sense of wholeness.

Direction and purpose have been primary benefits of my faith. And these stabilizing elements have often given me strength and insight when I have been faced with seemingly insurmountable obstacles or concerns.

The Scriptures

Not only can we have a personal relationship with Jesus Christ; we also have the Scriptures, God's inspired Word.

In my opinion, God did not intend the Bible to be a code book of specific moral laws covering every situation related to families or other concerns. Instead, the Scriptures provide us with vital, timeless principles regarding our actions, attitudes, and beliefs. These need to be worked out in specific situations in each generation.

The Scriptures also give us a historical record of how people throughout a long period of time dealt with dilemmas similar to those we face today—problems of priorities, conflicts with other family members, struggles with materialism, and so on. We can learn much from how these people dealt successfully—or sometimes unsuccessfully—with these concerns.

In a day when so many values are being called into question, people want a sense of certainty about what is right or wrong. This need can cause us to misread or misuse the Scriptures.

The Bible, then, is different from a law book you would find in a lawyer's office or a library. Certainly there are many specific rules in Scripture that are helpful for daily living. But more often than not, the guidance we receive from the Bible is in quite general terms —in helping people understand their need for God, in providing general standards for how we should think, feel, and act. And these standards, such as those found in the Ten Commandments or in the Sermon on the Mount, need to be carefully and faithfully related to today's concerns.

We cannot find God only through our feelings, thoughts, traditions, and consciences. We need God's Word to tell us about God—a source from "out there" that has authority, not a source inside ourselves that may be highly affected by our feelings and attitudes.

One of the most important but difficult tasks in using

the Bible is to tell the difference between what is eternal (designed for people of all times) and what was intended to relate specifically to the people who lived in the times the Scriptures were written. As we work at this task, we need to remember several basic guidelines:

• We should try to understand the original meaning and intent of the writer.

• We should look carefully at the historical context in which the Scriptures were written.

• We should allow the New Testament to interpret the Old, so as to give us an overall view of what God intends for us.

It is possible for a person to substantiate practically any point of view based on a reading (or misreading) of Scripture. Following the basic guidelines just mentioned can help clear up some of the ambiguities and help us resist the temptation to look for more in the Scriptures than God intended to be there.

The Holy Spirit

The Scriptures tell us that the Holy Spirit is a teacher, a guide, and a source of strength who not only gives insight but also the desire and courage to do what is good and true (see John 16:12-14).

Doing what is right is not always a problem of adequate knowledge or right feelings. We may know what is right, but lack the courage to do it (see Rom. 7:13—8:4 for an example of the apostle Paul's conflict).

As we live in a relationship with God, the Spirit is a motivator, stabilizer, and energizer in our lives.

Yet we must caution against the easy "leadings" and "urgings" that some people seem to experience with God. I do not question persons who say they have heard a voice from God telling them what to do. Yet in my own experience, there has rarely, if ever, been a clear, audible voice that has told me what to do. I have often sensed God's presence in the midst of incredible circumstances. But never has there been a bolt of lightning or voice that made a choice obvious.

We need to test these "leadings" (which *may* be God) against the teachings of Scripture. There needs to be a balance between the subjective, inner feelings we have (which may be raw feelings, intuition, conscience, or the voice of God), with the objective teachings of the Scriptures.

Finally

When it comes to making moral decisions about what is right or best, we have more than our senses of smell, taste, sight, sound, and touch to guide us. Imagine what a mess the world would be in if everyone acted only on their senses! (Unfortunately, that's about all some people seem to use!)

Everyone has the ability to think and feel. Traditions, intuition, and conscience also play a part in these dynamics. Christians have other sources of guidance at their disposal because of their faith in Jesus Christ: the teachings of Scripture and the Holy Spirit.

At the core of making decisions as Christians, then, is our relationship with Christ. The teachings of Scriptures give us guidelines of infinite value as we wrestle with problems and concerns today. And as we allow our faith to interact with our thought and feeling processes, we find that God's Spirit helps teach, mold, guide, and prompt us in a process of growth that hopefully results in making decisions of increasing maturity and depth.

Children, also, have all of these sources of guidance at their disposal. Even though their thought and feeling processes may be more immature than those of adults because of their development, children can also be great examples of the importance of trust and faith in the process of making decisions. Just as we need to seek ways to stimulate children to grow morally, we need to stop and observe ways they may already be implementing matters of faith from which we can learn and grow.

Your Turn

1. Reflect on how you make important moral decisions. Review the descriptions of sources of guidance available to everyone: traditions, reason, feelings, intuition, and conscience. What is your typical pattern? In other words, which of these sources of guidance do you find yourself using more than others?

2. If you are a Christian, reflect on how the Scriptures and the Holy Spirit are helpful to you. How do you experience God?

3. If you are not a believer in Jesus Christ or profess another religion, reflect on how your faith fits in with the development of morals and values. Write out your own statement of belief, a statement that describes in simple words how all this fits together for you.

6

What's the Bottom Line?

Over the years of human history, customs, styles, values, and morals have changed considerably. What is best, right, or true for one generation may or may not be the same for the next generation.

For example, in New Testament times, there was strict teaching about the length of women's hair and the need for their heads to be veiled—especially during worship. Yet men's heads were not required to be covered. The apostle Paul seemed to have some strong theological reasons why these customs were to be followed (see 1 Cor. 11:4-10).

For the most part, those customs are not universally accepted today. It is true that in some parts of the world women do keep their hair uncut and wear veils, but in Western societies, this has not generally been the case. I doubt that many women feel guilty when they get their hair cut.

Groups of people always develop codes of behavior that seem to them to be universal—in other words, each group believes its code should apply to everyone within its boundaries.

For example, just a generation ago the use of nylon stockings and lipstick by women was decried in many pulpits by ministers who felt that such "secular" customs were symbolic of our fallen nature and should be avoided at all cost.

Today one can enter the sanctuary of even the most conservative church and find women with contemporary hair styles, nylon stockings, and wearing various kinds of makeup.

Only a generation ago, beards symbolized the worst of hippiedom. Today beards are commonplace and seen on men in every part of the country (as well as on my own face!).

Does this mean that our generation has deteriorated morally? Not necessarily. But it does mean that at least some of the values people uphold to be "eternal" (true for all generations) may instead be "relative" (true at a particular time, but not forever).

The difficulty is in trying to tell the difference between these two kinds of values. What are eternal values, and what are merely cultural customs that will probably change next year or in the next generation?

I would like to suggest that there are several eternal values that the Scriptures clearly teach. From these values come important guidelines that can help us as we wrestle with problems and concerns unique to our generation.

Value 1: Focusing on God

At the core of life is the enjoyment of a relationship with God.

When asked by religious leaders what the most important commandment was, Jesus replied, "Love the Lord your God with all your heart and with all your soul and with all your mind" (Matt. 22:37).

As those who live in a personal relationship with God, we are called to commit our energies, thoughts, values, and aspirations to this one who has given us life and love. We live in grateful response to the God who has loved us in so many ways.

Over a period of time, it is possible—but not automatic—that persons who live in growing relationships with God find their self-esteem strengthened and painful memories healed, with renewed confidence to build meaningful relationships with other persons.

So why is it that in some there is, over a period of years, no evident change? Some people claim to be Christians for a lifetime, but seem to remain as critical or cranky or neurotic as ever.

I'm not sure I have a clear answer on that. But it does seem that for some people there exists a wall between themselves and growth, closing off potential for change and maturity. For some people, belief in God is an excuse for being judgmental, miserable, or close-minded.

For others, a relationship with God is a bridge to a new life—liberation from self-destructive patterns and loneliness, and the source of new purpose and hope for living.

Just what is the difference? I'm not entirely sure. But a key factor I have observed is a difference in attitude. For some people, belief in God is used to reinforce a life-style that already exists, no matter how miserable they are. For others, belief in God indicates a desire to grow and change, to experience fulfillment in life.

An attitude of being open to new understandings, willing to experiment with new behaviors, and allowing ourselves to be "stretched" with new attitudes is a key ingredient for growth to spiritual maturity.

As we live for God and enjoy a developing relationship with God, we need to ask: Do our thoughts, attitudes, and actions reflect our love for God? How can a relationship with God change us?

The Scriptures are full of descriptions of the personal qualities God desires us to develop. Our goal should be meekness, mercy, purity of heart, and peacemaking (Matt. 5:3-9). We are to concentrate on what is true, honorable, just, and pure (Phil. 4:8).

A life that centers on God is one that will clearly affect all dimensions of life—our thoughts, attitudes, feelings, behavior, needs, and concerns. To believe in God is to have a focus, a stable support, an anchor in facing the realities of living and dying. Even though there have been painful and seemingly insurmountable challenges, I personally find that I have a source of joy and stability that helps me cope, and which over a period of time has influenced my life to its core.

Before moving on, I'd like to issue one caution: to live life in a growing relationship with God is not necessarily the same thing as to be busy with church activities.

In some circles, people assume that if we are busy with "God's work" (that is, the work of the church), we show evidence of spiritual maturity.

Involvement in worship, education, and other church activities can certainly be vital for spiritual enrichment and growth. But church involvement is a *means to an end,* not an end in itself. For some people, the church becomes a fortress, a place to focus all of one's social energies, thus keeping one from having time for interaction and relationship building with people outside the church. Ironically, then, the church can become an escape from the realities of life.

There does not seem to be a correlation between one's involvement in the church and one's moral and spiritual maturity.

Seeking a proper *balance* is an essential task for all of us. Even as we seek to know God better (which may take place in our homes, churches, or wherever), we need to realize that this relationship does not become an end in itself, nor should church involvement absorb all of our energies.

The purpose of the church is to provide opportunity to worship, learn, and relate. It is a place to find inspiration and insight, to be encouraged and supported. But all of this is to be geared toward those outside the church. And that brings us to our second value.

Value 2: Orienting Ourselves to Other Persons

It is interesting to note that when Jesus was questioned by the religious leaders about the most important commandment, he quickly followed the command to love God with another: "And a second is like it, You shall love your neighbor as yourself. On these two commandments depend all the laws and the prophets" (Matt. 22:39-40).

In other words, to focus only upon a relationship with God (the vertical dimension) and ignore our relationships with ourselves and other people (the horizontal dimension) is to be incomplete or stultified.

God cares about all people. Human beings have been created in God's image, with the ability to reason, value, feel, and relate. God created us to be in relationship with others, to be person-oriented.

What exactly does this mean? Some people are more

75

oriented toward things than toward others. They focus on material possessions, status, or performance—what one has, or how one did.

A "thing-oriented" parent, for example, might focus on the importance of a child's winning or getting the best grades, at whatever cost. There may be little concern for how a child is feeling or even what is being learned. In that process the child may become an emotional casualty.

I remember such a person whom I knew during my first year of college. During our first semester he told me that unless he got straight As (in a school where very few persons ever got straight As), he would not be welcomed home for Christmas. The more he struggled to get top marks, the more nervous he became, and the worse he did. Finally, by Christmas, he could tell that his grades would be only average, and he spent the holidays away from his family.

I have often wondered since that time what has become of that young man, and what his relationship with his parents is like now.

We treat people like objects if we feel they can be manipulated and controlled. We treat them like persons when we care about them as individuals, when we take the time to understand their past and present concerns, their needs and feelings. We need to be flexible in our expectations, allowing for individual differences. We also need to treat people as equals, not as those who are beneath us or above us. We are all of equal value in the sight of God, and we should treat each other that way as well.

Thus, we should share rather than impose; accept rather than reject; seek to help rather than to control or manipulate; love rather than envy, resent, or hate.

But notice that Jesus said, "You shall love your neighbor as yourself." That has been interpreted in a number of ways. But it seems clear to me that Jesus is saying, "Love others in the same way [or as much as] you love yourself."

In other words, skills in relating to others are based on healthy self-esteem, on a realistic and grateful acceptance of ourselves, of our strengths and weaknesses, our successes and failures, our abilities and limitations.

To love ourselves is different from being conceited— the kind of "me first, no matter what the cost or at whose expense" attitude that is so prevalent in our society. Self-love implies a realistic acceptance and appreciation of oneself, but never at anyone else's expense.

We can give to others only what we possess ourselves. If we do not care about our own needs, or if we advance ourselves while others get hurt in the process, we have not learned the depth of truth Jesus has taught us.

Someone asked me recently, "How do I learn to accept others? I seem to hold them at arm's length and judge and criticize them." After listening to the person a while longer, I advised that the place to begin was with himself. It was evident that there was strong self-dislike, a denial of his feelings or needs, which he then projected onto others.

Even as we seek to help our children grow and develop, we need to remind ourselves—and them—that we have needs as adults as well. To ignore ourselves and commit all our energies to parenting (or to any other task, for that matter) is to burn out and thus lose our effectiveness.

Growing is a two-way street. If we always remain at the receiving end of love and attention, we become self-indulgent and spoiled. But on the other hand, if we are always at the giving end, we may burn out and become resentful and exhausted.

A balance between giving and receiving, nurturing others and nurturing ourselves, is the key to developing the kind of value system God wants us to have.

Value 3: The Centrality of Love

Throughout the Scriptures, we find that *love* is a key word appearing again and again. The kind of love God models for us seeks to nurture and care for others without expecting something in return.

So often in life, even in parent-child relationships, love can become conditional. I will love you *if* (you get straight As, you clean up your room, you finish your supper, and so on); or I will love you *when* (you love me first). Such conditions clutter our attempts at loving and base them more on performance than simply on the fact that we care.

Paul gives us some important characteristics of love: "Love is patient, love is kind. It does not envy, it does not boast, it is not proud. It is not rude, it is not self-seeking, it is not easily angered, it keeps no record of wrongs. Love does not delight in evil but rejoices with the truth" (1 Cor. 13:4-6).

That kind of mature, growing love takes a lifetime to develop. From the egocentric days of early childhood, through the growing pains of adolescence, through the crisis of adult years, such love is a challenge to express and maintain.

These three values overlap with and nurture each other. As we grow in a relationship with God, we receive insight and courage to reach out to others in love. As we seek to be person-centered rather than oriented toward things, we are more inclined to consider the needs, feelings, and concerns of others.

As we are loveable ourselves—enjoying and appreciating the efforts of others to love us—our own souls are nurtured. And as we are loving—sharing love with others and affirming them—we grow through giving.

Values in the Home

These values are the foundation for a healthy system of morals and values. Admittedly, they are quite general. But perhaps this is their greatest value, since they can be applied to so many situations and needs.

The home is an excellent place for us to implement these values, to practice them in our relationships with our children and other family members.

Your Turn

1. Reflect on the ways your values reflect the importance to you of a relationship with God, the importance of other persons, and the primacy of love in your life. Which of these key values reflects your "growing edge" (perhaps the area which is most difficult or challenging to you)? How can you strengthen your efforts in any of these three areas?

2. Apply these three key values to the following situations:

• Your child accidently breaks your favorite vase.

• Your child wants a friend to spend the night—a child you find to be rebellious and difficult.

• Your child repeatedly asks for drinks of water and hugs at bedtime.

• Your church asks you to serve on a board, the meetings of which will conflict with family activities.

3. Are you more of a giver or a receiver? What steps

can you take to maintain a better balance between the two?

4. Where are you in relation to your self-esteem? What can you do to enhance your own sense of self, even as you are seeking to enrich and strengthen the self-esteem of your children?

7

What Do I Do When Values Conflict?

One day in early November you remember that it is your turn to entertain all of the relatives on Thanksgiving Day.

With a sigh, you remember that you have started a new job within the past few months. What with the long drive, the use of new skills, and the adjustment to a demanding boss, you feel exhausted most of the time. The thought of getting up at six o'clock in the morning to get the turkey stuffed, do last minute cleaning, and get everything ready has your stomach in a knot. In fact, you are sure you would rather stay home alone with your children and have a simple dinner.

But the relatives are already asking what they can bring. After all, it's your turn. And could you in good conscience change the plans of all your relatives because you don't feel up to entertaining the whole group?

What would you do?

You have worked in your present job for over 10 years. You feel increasingly bored and unfulfilled. with your work. In fact, you feel so "stuck" that you dread going to work each day.

You have begun making inquiries as to other job possibilities. You have found a job in the computer field that sounds exciting to you. The problem is that it involves a year of additional training while you work at a lower salary.

What complicates the matter is that one of your children is ready to start college next year and needs your financial support for at least the next four years.

What would you do?

Your elderly great-aunt wants to live with you. You have been close to her for years. Now, because of some physical problems, she can no longer live on her own. Yet she doesn't want to move into a retirement home. She wants to live with family.

You know her moving in would put quite a strain on your family. Your two teenage boys would have to share a bedroom. And your home has only one bathroom.

But you are also concerned about your great-aunt, a person who has been helpful and encouraging to you since you were a child.

What would you do?

One of the paradoxes regarding decisions which involve values is that they are not usually matters of clear "rights" and "wrongs."

We have clear laws regarding some wrongs (such as murder and burglary) and rights (such as loving others and being peacemakers). But often we may feel caught with the "in-betweens"—those decisions in the "gray" areas of life that are not purely a matter of right or wrong. In fact, sometimes these places feel like "no-win" situations.

Take a look back at the situations described at the beginning of this chapter. The Thanksgiving dinner dilemma finds a person caught between personal need for rest and an extended family's expectation of a Thanksgiving dinner. No matter what decision a person makes, someone will be displeased or disappointed.

A person faced with a job change that involves a pay cut during an interim training period may find it difficult to have sufficient funds for a child going away to college.

And love for the elderly may come into conflict with the needs of one's own children.

Just how one deals with such complexities is the subject of this chapter.

Tragic Moral Choices

What makes moral decisions so difficult is that often they are not simply a matter of making clear choices between right and wrong. In fact, in some situations, persons may feel that they are choosing between the lesser of evils—called "tragic moral choices."

For example, a woman may find herself in a situation in which her spouse has been abusive on a number of occasions—not only verbally, but also emotionally and physically. Her husband has also been abusive with the children. He refuses to consider counseling, and threats to call the police seem to make him even more angry.

That woman is faced with a tragic moral choice: does she stay in a situation that is abusive to herself and her children, or does she leave her husband and consider divorce proceedings?

Consider another situation. You inadvertently find out that your teenage son is sexually active with his girl friend. You know that you could not prevent him from finding a way to be with her. You are also concerned that she could become pregnant. What do you do? Talk about it with your son and try to convince him to change his behavior? Urge him to use some method of birth control? Does encouraging the use of birth control methods imply that a parent is condoning the actions of the son? Or is it merely choosing the lesser evil in order that a more difficult situation can be avoided?

Secular Values

We do not live in ivory-covered towers, unaffected by the world around us. To believe otherwise is to deceive ourselves.

Instead, we are surrounded and inundated by conflicting values that reflect a variety of life-styles and beliefs. At the root of these conflicting values are several "isms":

- *Materialism*—the worship of things or possessions.

- *Narcissism*—the worship of self at the expense of other people—a "me first, no matter what the cost" attitude.

- *Atheism*—or godlessness—a belief system lacking any recognition of a supreme being.

Values based upon any of these "isms" could be called *secular* values. In other words, such values are indifferent to or reject the spiritual dimensions of life.

The apostle Paul described the kinds of attitudes and actions that reflect a secular attitude toward life (what Paul called "the acts of the sinful nature"): "sexual immorality, impurity and debauchery; idolatry and witchcraft; hatred, discord, jealousy, fits of rage, selfish ambition, dissensions, factions and envy; drunkenness, orgies, and the like" (Gal. 5:19-21).

The opposite of these attitudes and behaviors is what Paul calls "the fruit of the Spirit": "love, joy, peace, patience, kindness, goodness, faithfulness, gentleness and self-control" (Gal. 5:22-23).

Dealing with the "In-Betweens"

Not only are we faced both by subtle and obvious secular values that complicate our choices, but we are also faced with choices which are not always clearly right or wrong.

When faced with such dilemmas, you may find it helpful to ask the following questions:

What are the basic options in this situation? List them as clearly as you can. Think of more than two options if you can.

How will each option enhance or detract from my relationship with God? Do any of the options have clear implications regarding your relationship with God?

How will each enhance or detract from my relationship with other people? Will any option have impact on any of your family members? Your friends or neighbors? Business associates?

How will each option help me become—or keep me from becoming—the person God wants me to be? We need to consider our own concerns as well. Being concerned about ourselves can be quite different from the "me first" attitude some people have.

Are there any specific teachings in the Bible about any of the options? Be careful on this. People can easily read into the Scriptures what they want to hear and thus misinterpret the intent of the author. Let the Scriptures speak for themselves.

Are there any general principles found in the Bible that relate to any of the options? More often than not, you may find that the Scriptures do not have definitive, specific guidelines regarding your dilemmas. But there are many general principles that can help us make decisions. For example, "What are the implications of the Ten Commandments or 1 Corinthians 13 for the decisions we face?"

What are my feelings and motives concerning each option? Most of us find it almost impossible to be completely objective in making moral decisions. But work at stepping back, taking time to meditate and reflect. Just where do you stand with each option? What will you gain or lose with each? What do you really want?

How does my past experience influence each option? Do you have any biases or beliefs from your past that are affecting your decision making?

Give Me Time!

One of the greatest enemies to making clear-cut decisions is the pressure of time. We may feel we need to know *now* what we should do. But some decisions take longer than a few minutes to make.

Not long ago, I was faced with a difficult decision that called into question just about every value I had. The people pressuring me for a decision needed to know right away. But it seemed that the more I thought about it, the more confused I became.

So I asked for 30 days, figuring that if my decision was that important to those people, they could wait a month.

What a month that was! During one day, I would be sure that one option was "right" for me, having answered all of the questions stated above. But then the next day another option would seem much more "right."

The only way I could maintain any degree of sanity was to tell myself that it was OK not to know, that for the meantime I had decided not to decide.

On the 30th day the "right" decision for me emerged. I have never regretted making that decision, nor have I regretted having a month in which to ponder the alternatives.

But sometimes we may not have the luxury of 30 days. What then? I would suggest that you take as much time as is possible, even if it's only one hour. Our minds need time to ponder, think, and evaluate. Without time, we may feel like animals reacting to the whims of impulse.

Complications to the Process

If making right moral decisions were based only on knowledge, we would probably live in a more moral world (although ignorance is still quite a problem, even for people who think of themselves as learned!).

But there are some significant complications that may make us wonder if we will ever be able to make mature moral decisions:

Will Power

The apostle Paul frequently struggled with having the will to do what he knew to be right. Listen to his anguish: "I do not understand what I do. For what I want to do I do not do, but what I hate to do. . . . I have the desire to do what is good, but I cannot carry it out. For what I do is not the good I want to do; no, the evil I do not want to do—this I keep on doing" (Rom. 7:15, 18-19). Such struggle with our wills frequently points out the need for courage to put into action what we have seen or concluded is right, best, or good.

Attitude Problem

We need to reflect on the kind of attitude we have. Is it

an attitude that is loving, hopeful, and reconciling? Or is it angry, defensive, and bitter?

Our attitudes really do influence our beliefs and actions—they can be as souring as polluted water or as enhancing as delicate herbs and spices.

The Maturity Factor

In our earlier years, we may feel without a doubt that we know what is right or best. (As I reflect on my journals during my college years, I shudder at times in embarrassment at how simple life seemed to be, and how judgmental I could be with people who didn't seem to agree with me!)

The growing process has a way of helping us become more wise, all things considered. Wisdom does not automatically come with age. Attitudes, values, and coping mechanisms are among the factors that influence whether or not we become wise.

Self-Esteem

Poor self-esteem can affect a person in a number of ways. Some persons may convince themselves that since they are "not OK," no decision they make will be right. So they remain indecisive, sometimes until it is too late— and in not deciding, a decision has been made.

Other persons with poor self-esteem may have developed a defense which has them convinced that they are "always right." They make decisions quickly—even impulsively—and remain defensive toward those who question their wisdom or motives.

Healthy self-esteem, on the other hand, gives persons the basic confidence with which to deal with moral dilemmas. They have a realistic understanding that they are not always right, but that they do have the capability to wrestle with difficult issues and make decisions that will be right or best—even if it involves the choosing of "lesser evils."

Persons with healthy self-esteem are usually relaxed and realistic enough about themselves that they are free to fail, and thus more than likely will not be tied up in knots by the fear of failure. Instead, they will step out with courage and make what seems to be the right decision, knowing full well that one may never be entirely sure that the "right" decision has been made—especially in a world of "in-betweens."

Previous Experience

Some persons may have a history of poor experiences when it comes to decision making. Some of them had parents who made all the decisions for them. Others may have had experiences that made them bitter, afraid, or despondent. The stronger the negative feelings regarding these experiences are, the more difficult it would be to make adequate decisions in a similar area in the future.

Quality of Relationships

It is amazing how various factors affect our decision-making processes. For example, if I really like someone and feel close to that person, any decisions regarding that person will often be quite clear-cut. But if I am alienated from that person or have unresolved conflicts with them, my ability to be objective and consider what is right or best is greatly affected.

For this reason, we need to improve the quality of our relationships, even as we make important decisions regarding these relationships. Otherwise we may be speaking from a position in which our feelings are so clouded by anger or bitterness that we cannot make decisions that are wise or best.

Finally

Making moral decisions that are wise and best is really quite complicated. At times we may feel like withdrawing—putting our heads in the sand and thinking ourselves more safe there than in dealing with life's complexities.

But even though the process of making decisions may be complicated, it's not impossible. Especially not for those who are Christians. We have a foundation of beliefs that can guide and clarify matters for us. And all of these processes take place for us within the context of a relationship with a personal God who has promised to stay with us and not abandon us, who will help us develop the insight and courage to do what is best and right.

Your Turn

1. Read Galatians 5:19-23 again. Make a list in a column of all of the words that describe "acts of the sinful nature" and "fruits of the Spirit." Use a dictionary to find definitions for any words you may not be sure about. In the first section ("acts of the sinful nature"), cross out any words that are not problems for you. Underline those qualities with which you do struggle, those that are your "growing edge." Repeat the process for the "fruits of the Spirit."

Then list specific behaviors you will try to do in the coming week for any qualities you have identified as "growing edges," where you want to grow and change, especially in your family. Share your list with your spouse or a close friend. Talk together regularly regarding how your plan is progressing.

2. Reflect back to the time you were an adolescent.

What were some of the values conflicts you had with your parents? Were these conflicts a result of a difference in knowledge? Wisdom? Attitude? Or what? How were these experiences similar to or different from the values conflicts you have with your children today?

3. Identify a decision or value which you *know* is right—something you have thought about and are sure of what should be done—but which you have not been able to do. Reflect on what may be the complicating factor: Will power? An attitude? Maturity? Self-esteem? Previous experience? Quality of relationships? What needs to be done? How will you do it?

4. Identify a conflict you are facing that might involve a "tragic moral choice." Why does this seem like a "no-win" situation? Use the guidelines this chapter provides to work through the conflicts.

Part 3
Values
and the Family

Why are family patterns as unique as individual personalities?

How do family patterns get started?

Why are they so difficult to change?

How can a "closed" family become "open"?

What are typical barriers to becoming and being a healthy family?

What is "family environment"?

How does it affect the development of values?

How does being an example affect my children's values?

What effect do various leadership styles have on my children's values?

Is structured learning more influential than spontaneous, unstructured learning?

What are some guidelines for keeping "in touch" with my children?

What responses besides "yes" and "no" can I use when handling conflicts?

When is the best time to "let go" of my children emotionally and let them become independent adults?

8

What's Important about the Family Environment?

In my work as a counselor and teacher, I come into contact with many kinds of families.

One day, as I walked into my office, the atmosphere surrounding a family waiting to see me was so tense that you could practically cut it with a knife. Few words were said, but the constant glaring, rolling of eyes, sighing, or staring at the floor were such powerful messages that no words were needed.

As I tried to get various family members to talk, there was so little response I felt I was trying to pry open a sardine can with my bare hands! Only after many weeks of hard work did this family's members use words that would match their facial and body expressions.

In another family, communication was rarely direct but most often channeled through one of the children. For example, if the father wanted to tell the mother that he preferred to sit in the soft chair rather than the sofa, he would tell his daughter, "Tell your mother I want to sit in the chair"—even while the mother was standing right next to him! It was as if the mother didn't really exist.

And to make the situation even more tragic, the mother was a part of this communication system. She would reply through her daughter, "Tell your father that my back hurts and I want to sit in the soft chair." On and on the process would go, until the daughter finally burst out, "Stop it, all of you! I don't know what I am—a puppet or a person. Don't talk to *me* unless it's *me* you want to talk to!"

Another family—some friends of ours—show a different side of family life. They also are not very verbal, for they are quiet, rather shy people. But as soon as you walk into their home, you know that they are glad you came. There are smiles, hugs, and other expressions of closeness—not only with the guests, but among the family members themselves. There is a special quality of environment in a home such as this one, a place you know is a satisfying place to live.

Why is it that some of us are blessed to have been born and raised in homes where the caring and nurturing were evident, while in other homes, the hostility and frustration is such that family members need a lifetime to overcome the effects of such an upbringing?

Let's take a few pages to explain some of the reasons why families develop as they do.

Basic Family Patterns: Open and Closed

If asked the question, "When does a family begin?" most of us would say that it is when two people get married (although, admittedly, there are a variety of family forms today). If we accept this basic idea, then we see that two individuals who are quite different from each other have met, fallen in love, and committed themselves to being married.

Just as each of the two spouses is unique, so each marriage and family relationship is unique. Over a period of time, the couple communicates and behaves in certain ways that are repeated and thus become patterns. And these patterns can be healthy or unhealthy.

This family relationship (technically called a "family system") is not stagnant or unchanging. In fact, families may be affected by stresses and changes from outside of their relationship (such as a job change, war, or an economic depression), or stresses and changes within their family relationship (such as the birth of a child, the death of a family member, or the onset of puberty). In order to survive, families find it necessary to deal with these stresses and changes and will use unique patterns of relating in order to cope.

For example, in some families, angry feelings are handled openly and directly. They are acknowledged, expressed constructively, and eliminated rather quickly. Other families, by contrast, find it uncomfortable to deal with their angry feelings. They tend to ignore such feelings, or to express them in indirect ways such as sarcasm, put-downs, or silent withdrawal.

Patterns for handling feelings such as anger tend to become so ingrained that they may be quite difficult, if not impossible, to change.

If taken to an extreme level of dysfunction, a family may be so sick that one of the children or parents becomes a scapegoat—the one that family members blame as causing the family problems. That person (called the "Identified Patient") may be the person who "acts" out through bizarre behaviors what is happening in the family, and thus is the one who is brought in for counseling as having the problem.

What is fascinating is that when a child or adolescent is brought in for counseling, there is frequently some family dysfunction in the relationship as well, a dysfunction that may indeed be a root cause for what is happening to each of the family members, especially those identified as having the most significant problems.

Family researchers have found that there are two basic kinds of family systems: open and closed. We need to remember that this is not merely a matter of *either* open *or* closed. In fact, most families would probably find themselves somewhere in between on a continuum such as that shown below.

Closed	Open
FAMILY SYSTEMS	

But let me describe some basic qualities for each kind of family.

Open families, the healthiest kind of families, are warm, loving, and expressive of feelings. Close, loving relationships are highly valued. These families possess helpful skills for dealing with stress and change, skills that allow for flexibility, and they encourage change and see it as a sign of growth. There is concern for the self-worth of each of the family members. Communication is direct and clear.

Closed families, on the other hand, often resist change. There is usually more focus of power ("I don't care how you feel; I'm your father and you'll do it my way!") and performance ("What do you mean, you didn't get straight As! How stupid could you be?").

Communication patterns in closed families are often quite indirect—either through angry, attacking styles of relating, or withdrawing, backing away behavior. Messages are often exaggerated or distorted.

In healthy families, there is more than the absence of dysfunction. Instead, healthy families are learning the skills of communicating and nuturing and are using them in patterns that are beneficial to all the family members.

Barriers to Family Health

Becoming a healthy family is quite difficult. There are a number of impediments to developing such openness:

• A poor example from our parents of what an open family is like.

• Resistance from our children or spouses to having a healthier relationship. (Many people, especially those in closed family relationships, actively resist change. They see it as a threat to their identity rather than as an opportunity for growth.)

• Excessive stresses—both from outside of the family and from within it.

• Differing value systems. Some people value closeness and intimacy and will work to achieve it. Others do not value closeness and will either directly or indirectly sabotage efforts to become a closer couple or family.

• Poor previous experience. Attempts at being close may have been frustrated, so that people may be less open to trying again.

The Family Environment

The environment apparent in a home—the relational atmosphere or quality of relationships—usually has a deeper, more lasting influence on its members than does direct teaching.

Christian educator Catherine M. Stonehouse, in *Patterns in Moral Development,* supports this point:

> Some of the most important things in life are learned from the environment in which we live, without any direct teaching. Few people would set out to teach a child that he is stupid, a bother, and unimportant. But when adults insist on doing things for the child, fail to praise his accomplishments, deride him for his failings, sigh when he wants something, and never have time for him, the child learns the lesson well.[1]

Study after study has shown that the family environment is the most critical factor in affecting children's self-esteem, success in marriage and family life, and achievement in jobs. In fact, family environment—the quality of relationships within the family—seem to be more important than level of income, degree of intelligence, social status, or any other factor.

There are several qualities of the family environment that should be our goal: an environment that is *loving, empathic, just,* and *intellectually stimulating.*

Loving

Studies have shown a warm and loving parent will be imitated more than an unloving parent. And children who live in positive, accepting environments have been found to be more willing to learn and will generally be more positive and confident than children living in environments that are hostile or frightening.

Children who have positive self-esteem are usually from homes where they feel loved, wanted, and appreciated.

This bond of love encourages maturity in moral development, since children will more likely be guided by an inner sense of what should be done rather than by an external pressure to do something because of the promise of reward or the threat of punishment.

Expressing love through words and actions, as well as providing quality attention for each child, seems to have lifelong impact. For example, saying "I love you, Johnny. I'm glad you're you!" helps a child feel both worthy and loveable.

In feeling loved, children develop the emotional security and confidence to make decisions on their own. Moreover, accepting parents provide positive models with whom children can identify, models they will desire to imitate.

Children who do not receive such love and affirmation, on the other hand, often are driven by unfulfilled emotional needs and by pent-up hostility.

Empathic

Webster defines *empathy* as "the capacity for participation in another's feelings or ideas."

A morally maturing person is therefore one who has a developing awareness of the feelings and needs of others. There is a sensitivity to the consequences of personal behavior on others. A moral person is learning to consider the viewpoints of others in deciding the best or most moral way to act.

Kohlberg identifies this feeling of empathy as the most important contribution a family can make to its children's values.

Many researchers maintain that empathy can be developed at a fairly young age. Very soon in life, a person can begin to understand the difference between accidental and intentional acts.

Parents can talk with their children about the effects of their behavior on the family. For example, a parent could say to a child, "Johnny, when you throw that ball at your sister, it hurts her."

Parents can also guide children in making decisions

101

by encouraging them to consider the feelings of those who might be affected by their decision. For example, a parent could say, "Suzie, how do you think the other children will feel if you give out your party invitations to your friends in front of them?" Or, "How would you feel if you were treated this way?"

Children may also need to have their feelings clarified about circumstances that have affected them. For example, a parent could say, "Jeff, are you saying that you feel sad because your friend won't play with you?"

A loving relationship that is honest and open will provide opportunities for children and parents to discuss together how life's events affect them.

Just

A home that encourages love and empathy will also encourage justice—equal consideration for all family members. Children who are treated fairly are more likely to develop morally than those who experience constant injustice.

Admittedly, a young person's view of justice may be quite self-centered and related to rewards and punishments for themselves. A more mature person is able to see justice in terms of other persons.

In fact, as Christian educator Ted Ward notes: "Nothing has more influence on the development of moral judgment than participation in a just environment."[2]

There are many ways to create a just environment in the family:

• Respect the feelings and opinions of every family member.

• Be consistent in terms of rules or guidelines (no double standards).

• Encourage all family members to participate in making some family decisions, such as those regarding rules.

Intellectually Stimulating

As we have already learned, a child's growing mind is an important factor in the development of a sense of morality. Frequently dialogs with children about their opinions, feelings, and needs are critical for both intellectual and moral growth.

In discussing a concern with a child, a parent can ask: "How do you feel about this?" "What are other ways someone else might feel?" "How might your friend feel about this?" We need to encourage our children to "stretch" their thinking in learning to cope with life.

Books, magazines, records, school materials, and television programs can provide opportunities for discussion about important topics of concern. Creative activities such as drawing, painting, modeling with clay, cutting, or pasting also provide opportunities for interaction.

Finally

A home environment in which children are both loved and accepted, where they feel a sense of responsibility in helping the family function in a just manner, and where they are encouraged to grow intellectually, provides the best setting for the development of an adequate system of values. This environment can help families be the families God wants them to be.

Your Turn

1. On the continuum provided on the next page, write the word *then* on the line where you think your family of origin would find itself as to being *open* or *closed* (if necessary, review the section of the chapter regarding definitions). Then write the word *now* on the line where you think your family (spouse and children) would be

103

today. How would you account for this similarity or difference?

2. In the space below, jot down a specific way or two in which you will seek in the coming weeks to enhance your family's environment for these areas:

Loving

Empathic

Just

Intellectually Stimulating

3. When you have a few quiet minutes available with your family, ask about a situation in which someone had to make a decision between right and wrong (or share an experience you had). Explore together the different ways a person could act in this situation, and what each person feels would be the right decision.

9

What Does Modeling Have to Do with Values?

A father and his son are sitting watching television.

SON   Dad, can you help me with my reading?

FATHER   *(Silence.)*

SON *(louder)*   Dad, can you *please* help me with my reading?

FATHER *(without looking at the son)*   Huh?

SON *(louder)*   Dad, I really need help with my reading. Mrs. Johnson told me that I would fail reading unless I start doing my homework.

FATHER   Can't you see that I'm busy right now? Let's do it another night.

SON   *(Sigh.)*

The following week.

SON   Here's my report card, dad.

FATHER *(looking over the card)*   You got a C minus in reading? What happened?

SON   I don't know. I just don't like to read. It's boring.

105

FATHER   Well, you'd better work on it—and get at least a B.

SON   Can we read together right now?

FATHER   You know I always watch the news at this hour. How about another time?

SON *(glumly)*   Forget it. I'll do it myself.

FATHER   I just can't figure out why you don't like to read.

Next door, a mother and daughter are talking in the daughter's room.

MOTHER   Beth, your room is a disaster. How can you ever find anything? You've left dirty clothes all over— papers, books, even a dead goldfish. It's a wonder you even find a place to sleep.

DAUGHTER   Sorry, mom.

MOTHER   Well, start cleaning up right now. I'll be in the other room. *(She walks a few steps away.)*

MOTHER *(calling to Beth)*   Beth, have you seen my tennis shoes?

BETH *(calling back)*   No, mom. They might be behind the newspapers by the front door—or maybe under the pile of dirty clothes in your bedroom.

MOTHER *(with a surprised look on her face)*   Oh, well, yes. You know I've been busy—and well, maybe I should start cleaning up my own things.

Another family is driving over to Uncle Bert's for their monthly visit.

FATHER *(while driving)*   Why do we always have to go to Uncle Bert's on Sundays? It's so boring—and he's got such bad breath—and his house is always a mess. I'd much rather be home watching the ball game.

A few minutes later, the family arrives at Uncle Bert's home and walks up to the front door.

UNCLE BERT   Hi! Welcome! So good to see you again.

FATHER *(enthusiastically shaking Uncle Bert's hand)* Hi, Uncle Bert. Good to see you, too. You know how much we look forward to seeing you.

SON   Let's go home, Dad. I want to be with my friends. Let's go!

FATHER *(disapprovingly)*   Jeff, how can you say such a thing? You know how much we like to come here. You can play with your friends later.

SON   But, Dad, in the car you said . . . .

FATHER *(interrupting)*   Be quiet, Jeff. We *love* to come here.

SON   But, Dad, you said . . . .

FATHER *(in anger)*   Be quiet, Jeff. We're glad to be here. *(Dad turns to Uncle Bert.)* Well, you know how children are. Guess we won't be able to stay very long today . . . .

"Ouch!" you may say. Sometimes our children are our best teachers as they point out our inconsistencies as well as our strengths. And often our actions do speak louder than our words—which brings us to the subject of modeling.

Your Models

Take a few moments to relax, sit back, and think about your growing-up years. Bring to mind some of the persons who had the greatest influence on you. Were they your parents? Grandparents? Teachers? Neighbors? Friends?

What was it about those people that impressed you? What did you most admire about them? In what ways did they influence you? Reminisce about some of the special times you had with that person or persons.

Speaking for myself, I remember a number of people who had a great influence on me. But there are a few who come immediately to mind.

Grandma Larson was always a special person. Not only did I enjoy the homemade breads and cookies she frequently baked, but I appreciated the many times we had to talk. As I reflect back on our conversations, I was the one who usually did most of the talking, and she did most of the listening. (How different from the times when she would chatter at length in Swedish on the phone with her friends!).

Grandma accepted me where I was. There were few sermons and no put-downs. Her love was evident in the twinkle in her eyes and in the choked-up voice that usually could find few words to say to me.

We shared many times together. When I was troubled by making a choice of majors in college, or choosing a career, a wife, or whatever, it seemed that grandma was the person with whom I frequently conversed. She never told me what to do. Sometimes she said nothing at all. But her kindness and acceptance encouraged me to explore and understand the ambivalences I felt.

She's gone now, but I frequently think of her. I miss those chats we once had. She has made an indelible impression on my life.

Another person who greatly influenced me was Aunt Olga—not a "family aunt"—but a person who worked with children at our church and was known affectionately as "Aunt Olga."

Aunt Olga worked magic with children through the use of puppets. She also told dramatic stories with a voice that could move quickly from a soft whisper to a mighty roar and back to a whisper quicker than you could say "Aunt Olga."

But more than being an expert performer, Aunt Olga cared. She made all the children feel important.

How did I know she cared for me? She needed the tables in the dark, damp basement meeting room wiped clean early every Sunday morning—before 8:00 A.M., if I remember correctly. So my father would take me down to church every Sunday morning—often on winter days when it wouldn't even be light yet. I would stumble through the dark church until I got to the children's room. There I would take a damp rag and wipe the tables clean.

Within a few moments, Aunt Olga would be there. Her face glowed as she exclaimed, "Why, Jimmy, you do the best job of cleaning those tables I have ever seen. You are very important to me!"

Why were grandma and Aunt Olga important? They treated me like a person. No matter how menial the task, they helped me see the importance of my work. They helped me gain self-confidence. They encouraged me to discover the "Jimmy" that was hidden inside.

You as a Model

As a child, I often watched people around me—both adults and other children. I observed how they acted, how they treated each other, and how they treated me.

Over a period of time, I found that there were certain people I liked more than others, those I admired because of their attitudes toward other people. I tried to act like them.

If you have a young child, you have probably heard them talk to a doll or stuffed animal in the same tone of voice they just heard from you.

It can be almost frightening to realize that our children watch us that closely, with the X-ray vision of young intuition that can pierce right through the toughest veneer of pretense or phoniness.

Whether we like it or not, our children do observe and identify with us as parents, and in this way their values develop as well.

You? A model? You bet.

Webster defines *model* as "something set or held before one for guidance or imitation."

We don't say to our children, "Look at us! We've got our lives all put together. Act like us if you want to succeed!" That kind of arrogance is not a very good example.

Instead, our children quietly watch us every day—the way we relate to other persons; the way we handle our disappointments, anger, and fear; the way we talk about the neighbors; the way we do our income taxes. It is these patterns that create a strong image in the behavior and memories of our children.

Jesus as an Example

Jesus certainly was an excellent model during his years on earth. He could have given all his energies to speaking to large crowds from a distance, where few could see him up close or get to know him personally.

Instead, Jesus chose to be with his closest disciples for intense periods of time—sharing their lives together, eating, sleeping, traveling, talking, learning—in close proximity. In this way Jesus could teach his disciples through the way he lived as well as by what he said.

For example, Jesus stopped and talked with a Samaritan woman—whom Jewish law said he should avoid (John 4:7-26). He wanted children around him (Matt. 19:13-15). He allowed people to love him in lavish ways, such as anointing his feet with costly ointment (Luke

7:44-46). He associated with societal outcasts such as the tax collector Zacchaeus (Luke 19:1-10). Talking and relating were often more important to Jesus than tasks such as housekeeping chores (Luke 10:38-42).

And Jesus' approach worked. Investing in a small number of persons—who could hear him up close, and understand his teachings by seeing them expressed in action—resulted in a group of men and women who started a spiritual revolution that began to change the world after Pentecost.

Values and Living

We can teach and explain our values to our children in words, but our values will more likely be understood when they are "lived out" by persons with whom our children have a close, loving relationship, persons our children want to imitate.

Our homes are human relations laboratories, places where children and adults alike can observe and try out behaviors, sift through values, and become persons who are mature in their value systems.

The example we as parents provide is an exceptionally potent way to teach values.

Flip Flop

I should mention at this point that we can be negative examples as well. Because the home is really the first place where children have relationships and observe the values of other persons, they tend to imitate negative as well as positive patterns.

For example, if a parent handles anger by withdrawing and not dealing with it openly, a child may imitate those same patterns. Or if a person handles fears by withdrawing and becoming physically ill whenever there is a threatening circumstance, a child may imitate that pattern as well.

Treating other persons as "things" to be manipulated rather than as persons, or harboring resentments, or valuing money rather than relationships—whatever our patterns or values, children see these at work firsthand at home and will tend to imitate them in their early years.

As children grow older, they come into contact with more and more value systems, many of which may conflict with those expressed in our families. So as children grow through adolescence, they are faced with the increasingly difficult task of resolving conflicts between various values and putting together a system of values that works for them.

Watching our young people struggle in this process can be a difficult experience for us as parents.

Modeling and Leadership

An essential part of being an example and encouraging the development of healthy values is shown in the way we lead our children.

There are three basic styles of family leadership: *authoritarian, permissive,* and *democratic.* Depending on the situation, we may find ourselves using more than one style of leadership. At the same time, most of us may find that we tend to use one style more than others.

An *authoritarian* home is one in which decisions are handed down like military orders from parent to child, without the benefit of any discussion. There is little involvement of the child in family decision making.

Communication in an authoritarian home is often quite tense, or does not exist at all, as children try unsuccessfully to assert themselves and express their feelings and needs.

Authoritarian parents are often quite insensitive to their children and focus more on performance than on needs or relationships.

A *permissive* home, on the other hand, is not a better alternative. In such a home, parents are frequently involved with their own interests to such an extent that there is little time available for family members.

Children in permissive homes often strive to be close to their parents. But in these unsuccessful strivings, they "act out" their frustrations through rebellion or withdrawal.

There is usually little closeness and certainly little leadership in a permissive family. Children and adults alike seem distant from each other.

A *democratic* home is one in which persons strive for family closeness. The opinions and needs of every family member are taken into consideration. The children are frequently drawn into discussions in which family matters require mutual decisions.

Family researchers have found that such mutual sharing in appropriate family decisions enhance the child's self-esteem and positive feeling of involvement as a responsible family member.

There is frequent interchange in a democratic home. All family members are encouraged to share their feelings and opinions constructively. "Brainstorming"—in which a number of alternative solutions for a specific concern are brought up and listed before they are evaluated—is an important part of eliciting ideas from family members.

Again and again we find that the best ideas for solving a family problem may come from the children. In our preoccupation with the complexities of various concerns, we as adults may overlook the more simple—and really the best—alternatives.

Such discussions encourage in everyone a sense of being worthwhile.

Yet we need to point out that there is a difference between being *authoritarian* and being *authoritative*. God has called us as parents to be leaders in our homes. We have the authority we need to be the right kind of leaders for our children.

To be *democratic* is not to abdicate our authority. To abdicate our authority is to be *permissive*.

There may be times when we need to make decisions in our families without the participation of every person. Issues related to marital intimacy or discord would be examples. Not every concern is appropriate for a family discussion.

Finding the appropriate balance should be our goal—being firm and consistent, but also being loving and open as parents.

At the same time, we need to include our children in the process of decision making wherever appropriate. You'll be surprised how often the children *can* make helpful contributions.

Finally

As you reflect on the kind of model or example you are, keep the following in mind:

Identify your own values and how you are teaching them.

Think of how your way of relating to people and your way of handling your feelings affect those closest to you.

Remember that none of us is perfect. We all have areas that can use at least mild improvement. If you feel you have failed at times in being the kind of example your

114

children need, don't give up. Often they can look beyond our failures and inadequacies and see the intentions we really do have.

Keep talking with your children. Value their ideas and opinions. Include them in family decision making whenever possible.

Your Turn

1. Thank-You Notes

Write thank-you notes to any persons who significantly influenced you in your growing-up years. You may have to work hard to locate some of these persons, but it will be well worth the effort. Share in your notes a few memories you recall. These people may not even realize how they influenced you. Your note will probably be the highlight of their day (or year!).

2. Scripture Search

Read the following Scriptures. What were the values Jesus was modeling in each of these situations? In other words, what value was Jesus exemplifying through his behavior?

References   **Values Jesus modeled**

1. John 4:7-15

2. Matt. 19:13-15

3. Luke 7:44-50

4. Luke 19:1-10

5. Luke 10:38-42

3. Self-Evaluation

Identify and reflect on your style of leadership in the family. Generally speaking, would you characterize yourself as *authoritarian, democratic,* or *permissive?* What are times when each style might be appropriate? What changes would you like to make in the way you relate to your children?

10

Me, a Teacher?

As I think back to those persons who had an impact on me in my growing-up years, I would have to say that my teachers were among the most influential—some for the better, some for the worse.

In first grade, I had my first introduction to humiliation. One day while one group of children was reading with the teacher, the rest of us were to work quietly at our desks. After several minutes, I had completed my assignment and sat at my desk with nothing to do.

I noticed a pile of purple construction paper on the teacher's desk. To keep busy, I went up to the teacher's desk, took a piece of paper, and went back to my own desk. I proceeded to use a white crayon to draw several potatoes. About the time I finished my drawing, I noticed the cold stare being focused in my direction by the teacher. I sat up abruptly when I heard the shrill command, "Jimmy, will you please stand up and show the class what you have done!" With the sound of muffled snickers in the background, I stood up in front of the class to share my potato picture.

Needless to say, I was so embarrassed that I practically wet my pants. I had not realized that the paper had been carefully counted and rationed. I was sorry, embarrassed, humiliated, depressed—and I don't think I've ever drawn pictures of potatoes or used purple paper or a white crayon again!

But perhaps the greatest impact of that situation was the cold, icy stare of the teacher, a glare that said, in effect: "What in the world have you done? How could you be so stupid?"

Just thinking about that experience can turn my skin cold and give me a knot in my stomach.

Second grade was a much better year for me. We had just moved, so I went to a new school. My teacher was one of those beautiful, kind, loving teachers who could do no wrong. Her attitude always seemed to be, "Jimmy, you can do most anything you want in life. Just do your best."

I couldn't wait to get to school each day. Talk about a happy, loving, learning environment! She gave me hope that maybe I could succeed, that perhaps I wouldn't have to be a klutzy moron for the rest of my life.

Another memorable teacher was the one I had in fourth grade. While it seemed that the first teacher had taught through humiliation and the second through love and encouragement, my fourth-grade teacher taught through fear, the kind of fear that can make you swallow your words and produce temporary amnesia every time you were called on in class.

She wore heavy black shoes, the kind with thick heels tipped with metal. While we were working at our desks, she would prowl the aisles to be sure no one was daydreaming.

A particular sin, in her eyes, was to have one's foot in the aisle. Again and again she warned us of the serious consequences for this sin, but she was not specific as to what they would be. One day I found out.

Absentmindedly, I put my foot out in the aisle as I was working. Within a matter of seconds, the sound of a wooden ruler being cracked on my desk made me almost jump out of my seat in fear. What kept me anchored in my seat, however, was the teacher's heavy black shoe as she pressed her heel down on my foot. Waves of pain shot up through my leg and made me want to scream. But I knew that crying was another forbidden sin, so I gulped down my tears and tolerated the burning sensation in my throat. Needless to say, I have been conscious of where I have placed my feet ever since. And I've discouraged my wife from ever buying heavy black shoes with metal-tipped heels!

My sixth-grade teacher was in sharp contrast to the foot-crushing experience of fourth and fifth grade. (I forgot to mention that I was "privileged" to have the same teacher for two years!) My sixth-grade teacher was my first male teacher, a kind-hearted, creative teacher like the one I had in second grade. He made sure that everyone felt successful. He could be found at school early each morning and until after dark every afternoon. He always seemed to be available for conversations or help with difficult homework. In the classroom, he made every science lesson an exciting experience in discovery.

That year, just prior to entering the "jungle" of the junior high years, I learned many important lessons. Perhaps most important was the realization that *everyone* has the capacity to learn and grow, and that none of us needed to be satisfied with what we already knew. There was always more to learn. That lesson made an indelible impression on me as I set out on an up-and-down road through the years of adolescence and into adulthood.

Me, a Teacher?

Take a few moments to reflect on your own experience with teachers. I'm sure that at least one or two will stand out in your mind as making some kind of strong impression, whether good or bad.

But whether the teachers were stern and scary, or competent and kind, you probably treated them with respect, as people who knew more than children did and who were there to help you learn.

Have you ever thought of yourself as a teacher? Maybe that's your profession, or perhaps you serve as a volunteer teacher at your church or community organization.

That's not exactly the kind of teacher I'm referring to. All parents, no matter how many children they have or how many years of parenting they have experienced, are teachers of their children. As we have already noted, parents teach their children many of the most important lessons regarding love and life beginning right from the birth of each child.

Kinds of Learning

When you think of teaching and learning, what comes to your mind may be the kind of formal or structured learning that is done in a classroom, in which an adult teacher guides children through learning experiences.

Certainly that kind of teaching and learning can happen in the family, through structured discussion or activity or the enjoyment of a story together. Some families actually set aside a special evening every week that they call "Family Time," when such learning can take place.

But there is much other learning that takes place in the family as well, what I call *informal* or *unstructured* learning. Such learning may be like that done on a field trip—learning by doing, discovering, and interacting. In the family, informal learning takes place continually throughout the day, while family members are eating, doing chores, doing dishes, playing games, doing homework, relating to neighbors or relatives, or in response to an unexpected happening to a family member (such as an accident, job loss, illness, or death).

The Scriptures talk about both kinds of learning. In Proverbs, we read of the more formal type of instruction that parents were expected to do with their children (Prov. 1:8; 4:1-4).

But we also find that the Scriptures encourage the informal kinds of learning that take place more spontaneously throughout the day (Deut. 6:4-9).

Let's describe in a little more detail how each kind of learning takes place in the family.

Unstructured Learning

Practically any situation in the family provides the opportunity for learning and growth to take place, whether it's a family event such as the birth of a child, death of a relative, moving, or an experience a family member has with others—such as a conflict with a friend or teacher at school, or problems with homework.

Informal learning can take place practically anyplace, while eating a meal, doing chores together, riding in a car, hiking, or playing a game.

We as parents need to take advantage of these informal moments for relating and learning. As we said in the chapter on enhancing the family environment, there is great value in using communication skills in these informal situations. Asking questions and drawing the children into dialog regarding their ideas and feelings are examples of how parents can enhance informal learning.

In these spontaneous moments, children can help *us*

learn as well. They can help us grow up even as we guide them (Matt. 19:13-15). Even our observance of our children's simple faith and trust can be an inspiring example.

I'll never forget the informal learning that took place soon after the death of my wife's grandfather. He had been dearly loved by all of us, so we felt a deep sense of sorrow and loss at his death, even though he had lived a long life.

The critical moment of learning took place one night as we were chatting after dinner. My youngest daughter, who was about three years old at the time, asked me, "Daddy, where did Pappa (her name for grandpa) go?"

"Well, Jodi, he went to heaven to be with Jesus," I replied.

After a few moments of silence, she said, "But, if he went to heaven, why did they put him in a box and put him in the ground?"

The conversation continued for several minutes with all three of my children. We all cried and shared how much we missed our Pappa. And after it was over, I realized how much my children's faith had touched me and helped me with my grief.

Several years later, I was reminded once again how much my children were helping me "grow up." I unexpectedly lost my job right before Christmas. I felt both shocked and devastated. I hardly knew how to share the news with my family.

But that night at dinner, as we quietly reflected together on what had happened, my children reassured me that we would be all right, that something even better might come along. Then one of my children offered to give up her allowance for a while if that would help! Rarely has our family felt closer or more committed to each other.

Learning through such events takes place in response to unplanned experiences in our families. They cannot always be anticipated or structured. But we need to remain sensitive to how such events can help every family member grow in understanding and faith.

Even though informal learning may often be quite spontaneous, we need to include times in our busy calendars so that such learning can take place more regularly.

Structured Learning

Many families find that they enjoy having a regular structured time together. Whether it is a Saturday breakfast, a Sunday afternoon, or a weekday evening, it is a time when all family members agree to be at home and spend some quality time together.

A Family Time may begin—or end—with a special meal that all family members prepare and enjoy together. Perhaps a favorite family activity such as a game is included. And there is often time for study and discussion of a particular subject.

A creative project using materials such as clay, crayons, felt pens, construction paper, and so on may also be part of a Family Time. There are a number of books that describe excellent Family Time activities (see the "Resources" section at the back of this book for suggestions).

In such learning, shared leadership—with each family member taking a turn—can maximize the experience. Children and young people will grow in their self-worth and confidence as they have opportunity to share in the leadership of these Family Times.

One of the greatest challenges regarding Family Times

is to find a time when all family members can be present. You may find it almost impossible to find an evening that is consistently free from week to week. Putting this commitment on the family calendar may be necessary, so that all family members will be together.

Quality: The Best Kind of Time

The key word I want to use to describe the kind of time we need together as families is *quality*.

With the rapid pace of living that many families find themselves involved in today, family time may be relegated to time in the car spent racing from activity to activity, gulping down quick meals, or sitting in varying states of exhaustion staring at the television set.

Some families find that they can live together for weeks, months, even years and have very few moments together sharing, communicating, listening, enjoying, and loving. But that is what quality time requires.

Quality time cannot always be structured, although Family Times can certainly help. Family relationships need to be top priority during the growing up years of our children. When we are able to do that with our actions, as well as with our words and intentions, we will begin to say no to other options without feeling guilty.

I have also found that a quantity of time is often necessary to ensure that quality time takes place. Without spending concentrated periods of time together, the spontaneous moments of quality sharing may never take place.

Unless we intentionally make time for our families a priority, we will continue to live with the "tyranny of the urgent"—responding to various demands for our

124

time, until there is little or no energy or time left for enhancing healthy family relationships.

Develop Your Own Style of Teaching

For many years families with a religious persuasion were urged to have what has been called "family devotions"—often a brief time of reading the Scriptures or a devotional book and praying together.

I've often wondered why certain families seemed to be successful with this kind of activity and others did not.

My guess is that there are many parents who have been urged to have "family devotions" who feel quite guilty because of their lack of success.

As far as I am concerned, just as there are no two individuals who are exactly alike, there are no two parents who relate to their children in exactly the same way. In some families, a structured experience of reading and praying can be productive and helpful.

But perhaps in other families, those in which the leadership style is more informal, the model of "family devotions" just won't work. Focusing on more informal activities, and still using conversation as a means through which to influence our children's moral and spiritual growth, can also be effective.

As was mentioned in a previous chapter, our greatest influence on our children is through our example. If our motives are right and we sincerely love our children, we will be teaching our children many important lessons as we grow as families and relate to the daily circumstances that influence all of us.

One other thought. If you are the parent of a young child, the time to begin structured activities may be when your child is still young. As creatures of habit, children enjoy the repetition of songs and activities that become part of the family traditions.

You will run into less resistance and more enthusiasm if you inaugurate Family Times during your children's early years. Resistance and indifference seem to be at their peak during children's adolescent years.

You? A teacher? You bet! Through your attitudes, words, habits, and feelings, you are teaching many important lessons to your children regarding life, faith, and love.

Your Turn

1. Plan a time to sit down with your family to discuss family activities for the coming months (3-6 months, depending upon how far in advance you want to plan). Have a family calendar available. As a family:

Brainstorm (listing without evaluating) the kinds of informal activities your family would enjoy.

Select activities that are realistic as to interest, cost, and length of time needed. Decide how often your family will schedule in such an activity. (Remember: activities can be at-home types which include making popcorn or fudge, looking at old family slides or movies, and so on.)

Calendar in these activities on specific dates so that everyone can plan around them.

Enjoy the activities your family has selected.

Evaluate your time together and decide together which activities you would like to repeat.

2. Talk with your family regarding the possibility of having a regular *Family Council* meeting. A Family Council is a way to involve our children in dealing with family concerns and making decisions that affect every

family member—such as chores, responsibilities, irritations, and problems. Whether weekly, biweekly, or monthly, such an event will probably need to be scheduled in so that every family member can be present.

At the beginning of a Family Council meeting, work together to develop an agenda (list of what needs to be discussed). Then deal with each item together, being sure that everyone is encouraged to express feelings and options about these family matters.

11

But What Do I Do When . . .?

Let's pretend for a moment that we can sit down together and talk about whatever concerns you still have, now that you have finished reading the preceding chapters. We have just filled our coffee cups and settled down into two comfortable chairs for a chat.

After a moment of silence, you begin: "Jim, I think I have a pretty good understanding of what you are saying. I understand how important values are, and I see now how the growth process influences people's values."

I interject, "Do you also see how important you are as a parent regarding your children's developing values?"

"Certainly. In fact, sometimes I get kind of scared to realize what a responsibility it is to be a parent. But I realize that my faith in God is an important factor that helps guide me and provide some basic values."

"Why do I think that the word *but* is about to be used?"

"You're a step ahead of me, Jim. Let me finish. I've really worked hard at providing the kind of loving home where my children could grow and develop the kind of values and morals that will help them."

There is a brief pause in the conversation, during which time I sense that you are still struggling with some unanswered questions.

"But, what?" I ask.

"I'm having a hard time putting my feelings into words," you say. "But what do I do when my children keep making decisions that I strongly believe to be wrong, whether it's associating with kids who keep getting into trouble, or skipping school, or not doing chores?"

"I get the picture. You're still frustrated by what's happening with your children."

"That about sums it up. I'm still not sure what to do when we hit those 'stuck' points when nothing seems to work. Usually we get so angry at each other that someone ends up yelling, stomping out of the room, and slamming a door. Then we hardly talk with each other for hours or days at a time."

"Those are discouraging moments in parenting, aren't they?"

If you identify with these comments, I can understand your frustration. I have been there more than once as a parent, and I expect to have such situations happen again before my children have grown up and left home.

Let me share a few concluding thoughts with you about what to do when there seem to be no easy answers, when you and your child feel "stuck" when dealing with a situation involving values or morality.

Communicate Regularly

There can be a tendency as our children grow older to ease off on communicating with them. In their earlier years, our children usually wanted to keep in touch and talk quite often. But as children enter the adolescent years, they are increasingly preoccupied with friends, school, and other activities, as well as with an intense concern with their appearance and growth. All of this means that children's energy that once may have been directed to communicating with parents is now being directed in many other directions.

Research has found that most teenagers do indeed still feel close to their parents throughout their adolescent years, and a very small percentage feel totally alienated from their parents for any length of time.

The key factor seems to be the parent's ability to keep in touch, to go the extra mile in being sure that the family relationship keeps developing. Assertiveness may be necessary to be sure that there are at least occasional meals together and other times when communication can take place.

Family relationships don't get nourished very easily if the only communication is a series of notes taped to the refrigerator. Direct, quality interaction is essential.

Be Involved and Interested in Your Children's Activities

One of the ironies of life is that just as our children grow to the point where their energy is taking them in many other directions than home, many parents are also involved in growth processes of their own, whether it's mid-life transitions, job changes, women returning to the job market, or adjusting to the reality of dealing with elderly parents.

Again, as we've said many times already, our values as parents need to include time for our children. Whether it's driving your child and friends to sporting events, occasionally volunteering to help in the classroom, or opening your home for a party for your children's friends, the time involved (and at times the inconvenience to your own schedule) will be well worth the effort over the course of a lifetime. You are in the process of building a scrapbook of memories that will strengthen the bond between you and your children for a lifetime.

Be sure that your children's special events are scheduled in as well, so that they remain a priority whenever possible.

Be Sure that Both Parents Are Involved

If you are part of a two-parent family, be sure that both of you stay in touch with your children. In many families, roles and expectations develop to the point where unfortunately one of the parents feels responsible for being the primary communicator with the children.

Have you ever heard your spouse say, "I just can't talk with him (or her) anymore. You'll have to be the one to keep talking"?

That's a very critical point in a family's relationship. Whenever either a parent or a child begins to withdraw from the relationship, problems tend to intensify. No matter how frustrating a family experience is, stay in touch.

This is true even if two parents have separated or divorced. As often as possible, both parents should seek to stay close to the children. This may involve overcoming some personal hurts or resentments felt toward the other spouse. But your efforts to lay aside that grief and maintain a close relationship with the children is one of the most important tasks you will ever accomplish.

Two parents working together can support and encourage each other, especially at those times when the parent-child relationship is strained or feels nonexistent.

Be Flexible

When relating to children, or anyone for that matter, we need to remember that we are not always right and we need ideas and input from others.

You may find that it is easy to give a quick no to something your child asks about without carefully thinking through what the request is all about. Save your *nos* for the important times, when you do feel quite strongly about a particular issue. At the same time, be flexible enough to be reasonable and considerate regarding your children's needs and wishes.

Occasionally you may find that you thought you were right about a particular issue, but on second thought, or after a period of time, you realized that indeed you were wrong and your child was probably more correct. At times like that, be sure to say you're sorry and ask for forgiveness. Nothing restores a relationship better than when people have owned up to their shortcomings and want to be reconciled.

Parents are not always inherently right, even though we may wish we could be! And apologizing to our children at those times when we have said something or acted in an inappropriate way is an unforgettable example for our children to observe and to imitate.

Sharpen Your Negotiating Skills

As I've already mentioned, many moral and value-related issues are not simple matters of rights and wrongs. Many times, issues are of the "in-between" kind, and there may be strong feelings attached to the opinions held on both sides. In fact, sometimes feelings can develop that are so strong that communication is stifled. Then family members may feel that the others don't really care about their feelings or ideas.

An important communication skill to develop is the art of negotiating. The goal of negotiating is to minimize the times that family members feel that someone has won and someone else has lost. A power struggle almost inevitably leads to feelings of being demoralized for those who feel they lost.

Families can benefit from working with a negotiating process to help them work through some of their differences—a process that seeks to help each family member identify what is being felt and to find areas of compromise wherever possible.

The beginning of the negotiating process involves an agreement between parent and child that a structured time of discussion needs to take place regarding a particular issue. (This process works best with older children and adolescents.)

The structure can work something like this:

Phase 1: Getting Started

Make a copy of the following pages, one copy for each person. Both parent and child complete the appropriate worksheet. Take as much time as is needed for this phase—at least 15 minutes will be needed.

Phase 2: Exploration

When both parent and child have completed their worksheets, they read what the other person wrote. Time is spent identifying which alternative or alternatives both persons can accept.

133

Phase 3: Decision

Decide together which alternative you will accept together and try. Again, remember that a spirit of willingness to compromise and as much objectivity as possible will be needed. If tempers flare, or if the tension is such that little progress is being made, agree to postpone the discussion until both parties can talk more objectively. But don't use postponement as a way to avoid the issue. Agree to a specific time and place for the next discussion.

Phase 4: Evaluation

At a later time, evaluate the alternative which was selected, especially if the issue comes up again. Have you both been satisfied with what happened? Should another alternative be tried? How has this process affected the parent-child relationship? How have your skills for communicating and negotiating been affected by this process?

Worksheet for Working Through Differences in the Family

Check one: I am   _____the parent

                 _____the child or adolescent

Briefly describe the issue as you see it.

What specfic areas for compromising are there?

List three alternatives you think would resolve the issue.

1.

2.

3.

Kinds of Responses

In dealing with issues that have become real conflicts, there are several ways to respond.

Wait

If feelings are so intense that any kind of reasonable discussion is impossible, I would suggest that persons wait until such time as they can be reasonable. We hope our families will not be run by the person who has the most dramatic tantrum or loudest outburst, but by those who can in reasonable fashion consider all sides of the difficult dilemmas which people both young and old face today.

When children and adolescents learn that decisions will not be made in the midst of angry screaming but will have to wait until people are in control of themselves and their emotions, they will learn the value of a more rational approach.

Say No

I wish I had an authoritative list of times a parent should in fact say, "No, I'm sorry, you just can't do that. In this situation, as long as you are living here with us, you'll have to do it my way. I'm concerned enough about you to set limits that seem to me to be fair for all of us."

Compromise should be the goal as often as possible, but there just may be times when that is impossible.

I do believe that there are times when a parent needs to be a strong leader—not overbearing, unyielding, and arbitrary, but assertive, direct, and loving. Both firmness and consistency need to supplement flexibility and openness.

Save your *nos* for those few times when there seems to be absolutely no way to compromise, when you feel strongly that if your children were to make a particular choice they would be doing irreparable harm to themselves, as well as to others.

Say Yes

There may also be times when your children will learn best by living with the consequences of their decisions. You will have to be the judge of how serious the issue is as you talk together with your children. But I have found that the learning and growing process is enhanced as children feel they can make at least some decisions for themselves, even if you don't agree with their particular choice and know what the results might be.

To use each of these responses wisely—*wait, no,* and *yes*—is to become a parent who is growing in capability as a parent. No single answer is always appropriate, especially regarding the "in-betweens" of life.

Hanging in There

There may be times when you feel like giving up, when all hope seems lost and there are just no more options. Especially in times like those, remember that you can believe in a God who has promised not to abandon you, no matter what happens. Faith in God can bring you hope, peace, and strength.

And there may also be a need for a third person to help. Certainly this has been true for us as a family. Sometimes we get so involved in a particular issue that it festers and grows in its intensity. Seek out the help of an experienced pastor or a family counselor trained to deal with such matters.

Many of us would immediately go to a doctor if we experienced pain in our bodies, but we may be hesitant to seek out professional help if our relationships are in pain. Believe me, I know from our own experience as a family that an objective outsider can be most effective in helping to clarify issues and solve problems. Take advantage of the help which is available in your community.

Letting Go

An irony of parenting is that one of our goals is to work ourselves out of a job. Even though we may feel parental concern for our children throughout their lives, we need to aim towards our children being emotionally independent from us, so that they can become fully functioning adults in their own right.

This letting-go process is more difficult for some parents than others. Having children meets certain needs in our own lives, and we may experience quite an adjustment process, including feeling disoriented or lonely as they leave home.

But our own abilities to let go and encourage our children to grow up will be an important indication of our abilities as parents. Parents who hang on or make the leaving process difficult for their children will need to deal with whatever underlying feelings are making this process so difficult.

But a time for letting go does come. Letting go may occur when children go away to college, move into their own apartment, or get married. Or it may be a process which takes place over a period of time, when a parent needs to feel, and maybe even say, "I've done the best I can. I've given you all the love and care I know how to give. I have failed at times, and I have succeeded at others. I will always love you and be grateful for the years we had together. I hope you will always love me. I know we haven't always agreed. But through it all I have cared for you. My thoughts, prayers, and love are with you as you leave. The rights, wrongs, and in-between with which we have struggled and grown are now your issues. You're on your own now to make your own decisions."

Your Turn

1. Use the "Worksheet for Working Through Differences" with your child in handling a current issue. How does the use of this kind of structure affect the way the two of you relate to each other?

2. Make a covenant with yourself to keep growing and developing as a parent. Here are a few suggestions to explore:

• Explore the possibility of taking a parent-education course in your community through your church, community college, YMCA, or wherever. If nothing seems available, suggest to one of these organizations that such a course would be of great interest to you. One of the best courses is called *Systematic Training for Effective Parenting*, a complete curriculum with materials for both leaders and parents (see the "Resources" section for details).

• Select a few books which will guide you in your own growing process as an adult. Join a group, if such is available, for people who are involved in a process similar to yours. Again, your church, college, or other community organization may have such opportunities available for you. If not, you may want to get something started on your own.

• Consider starting a Parent Support Group, a small group of parents who would like to meet for learning, sharing, and supporting each other as parents. The use of a book such as this one can be a stimulus for discussion. If a less structured group is desired, parents could participate in a more open-ended discussion of current concerns and issues.

Postscript

I hope that the reading of this book has stimulated your thinking, stretched your understanding regarding values and morality, and encouraged you to try some new behaviors as a parent.

Few of us are trained adequately for being parents before our children are born. We learn and grow as parents just as our children grow up. With each new age and stage, we are stretched as parents to develop new skills so that we are not just coping but also can enjoy the entire process.

There may be unresolved questions or dilemmas which you had hoped that this book would address. I would encourage you to write to me in care of the publisher if there is any concern you would like to share with me. I will get a reply to you as soon as the publisher forwards your letters to me.

My best wishes are with you as we all live together with our families in a world of in-betweens.

Notes

Chapter 1   What's Developing?

1. Jean Piaget, *The Origin of Intelligence in Children*, 2nd ed. (New York: International Universities Press, 1952).
2. Lawrence Kohlberg, "The Cognitive Developmental Approach to Moral Education," *Phi Delta Kappan* (June 1972), pp. 670-677; "Education, Moral Education, and Faith," *Journal of Moral Education* 4, No. 1 (1974), pp. 5-16; "Moral Education for a Society in Moral Transition," *Educational Leadership* (October 1975), pp. 46-54.

Chapter 3   Am I Really Important?

1. Kenneth Kenniston, *All Our Children: The American Family Under Pressure* (New York: Harcourt Brace Jovanovich, 1977), p. 17.
2. Ibid., p. 75.
3. Virginia Satir, *Peoplemaking* (Palo Alto, Calif.: Science & Behavior Books, 1972), p. 197.

Chapter 4   What Are My Values?

1. Ted Ward, *Values Begin at Home* (Wheaton, Ill.: Victor Books, 1979), pp. 13-15.

Chapter 5   What's Our Guide?

1. Gordon Allport, *The Individual and His Religion* (New York: Macmillan, 1962), p. 90.

Chapter 8   What's Important About the Family Environment?

1. Catherine M. Stonehouse, *Patterns in Moral Development* (Waco, Tex: Word, Inc., 1980), pp. 50-51.
2. Ward, p. 75.

141

Resources

Moral Development and Values

Larson, Jim. *Teaching Christian Values in the Family* (a 13-session parent education course). Elgin, Ill.: David C. Cook, 1982.

McGinnis, Kathleen and James. *Parenting for Peace and Justice*. Maryknoll, N.Y.: Orbis Books, 1981.

Richards, Lawrence O. *A Theology of Christian Education*. Grand Rapids, Mich.: Zondervan, 1975.

Stonehouse, Catherine M. *Patterns in Moral Development*. Waco, Tex.: Word, 1980.

Ward, Ted. *Values Begin at Home*. Wheaton: Victor Books, 1979.

Parenting

Briggs, Dorothy Corkille. *Celebrate Your Self: Making Life Work for You*. Garden City, N.Y.: Doubleday, 1977.

Briggs, Dorothy Corkille. *Your Child's Self-Esteem*. Garden City, N.Y.: Doubleday, 1970.

Ketterman, Grace and Herbert. *The Complete Book of Baby and Child Care for Christian Parents*. Old Tappen, N.J.: Fleming H. Revell, 1982.

Klein, Carole. *How It Feels to Be a Child*. New York: Harper Colophon, 1975.

Lerman, Saf. *Parent Awareness*. Minneapolis: Winston Press, 1980.

Levinson, Daniel J. *The Seasons of a Man's Life*. New York: Alfred A. Knopf, 1978.

Oraker, James. *Almost Grown: A Christian Guide for Parents of Teenagers*. New York: Harper & Row, 1980.

Pringle, Mia Kellmer. *The Needs of Children*. New York: Schocken, 1975.

Satir, Virginia. *Peoplemaking*. Palo Alto, Calif.: Science and Behavior Books, 1972.

Uslander, Arlene S., Caroline Weiss, and Judith Telman. *Sex Education for Today's Child*. New York: Association Press, 1977.

Parent Education Resources

Dinkmeyer, Don and Gary D. McKay. *Systematic Training for Effective Parenting*. Circle Pines, Minn.: American Guidance Service, 1976.

Griggs, Donald and Patricia. *Generations Learning Together: Learning Activities for Intergenerational Groups in the Church*. Nashville: Abingdon, 1976.

Larson, Jim and Jill. *Celebrating Togetherness*. Chicago: Department of Christian Education, the Evangelical Covenant Church of America, 1973.

Otto, Herbert A., ed. *Marriage and Family Enrichment: New Perspectives and Programs*. Nashville: Abingdon, 1976.

Sawin, Margaret M. *Family Enrichment with Family Clusters*. Valley Forge, Penn.: Judson Press, 1979.

Family Activity Resources

Braga, Joseph and Laurie. *Children and Adults: Activities for Growing Together*. Englewood Cliffs, N.J.: Prentice-Hall, 1976.

Sloane, Valerie. *Creative Family Activities*. Nashville: Abingdon, 1976.

Wilt, Joy and Terre Watson. *Seasonal and Holiday Happenings*. Waco, Tex.: Creative Resources, 1978. (There are a number of other excellent activity resources in this "CAN-MAKE-AND-DO" series.)